A-Z WARRINGTON

C000293241

CONTENTS

In...
Vi...
se...

REFERENCE

Motorway	**M6**	Car Park (selected)	**P**
A Road	A574	Church or Chapel	†
Proposed		Cycleway (selected)	
B Road	B5212	Fire Station	■
Dual Carriageway		Hospital	**H**
One-way Street		House Numbers (A & B Roads only)	13 8
Traffic flow on A Roads is indicated by a heavy line on the driver's left.	→	Information Centre	**i**
Restricted Access		National Grid Reference	350
Pedestrianized Road		Police Station	▲
Track / Footpath		Post Office	★
Railway	Station / Tunnel / Level Crossing	Toilet: without facilities for the Disabled / with facilities for the Disabled / for exclusive use by the Disabled	▽ ▽ ▽
Built Up Area	PRIORY ST	Educational Establishment	
		Hospital or Hospice	
Local Authority Boundary		Industrial Building	
		Leisure or Recreational Facility	
Posttown Boundary		Place of Interest	
Postcode Boundary within Posttown		Public Building	
		Shopping Centre or Market	
Map Continuation	20	Other Selected Buildings	

SCALE

1:15,840 4 inches to 1 mile   **SCALE**   6.31 cm to 1 km   10.16 cm to 1 mile

0	¼	½	¾	1 Mile
0	250	500	750	1 Kilometre

Copyright of Geographers' A-Z Map Company Limited

Head Office:
Fairfield Road, Borough Green, Sevenoaks, Kent TN15 8PP
Telephone: 01732 781000 (Enquiries & Trade Sales)
01732 783422 (Retail Sales)
www.a-zmaps.co.uk

Edition 3 2005

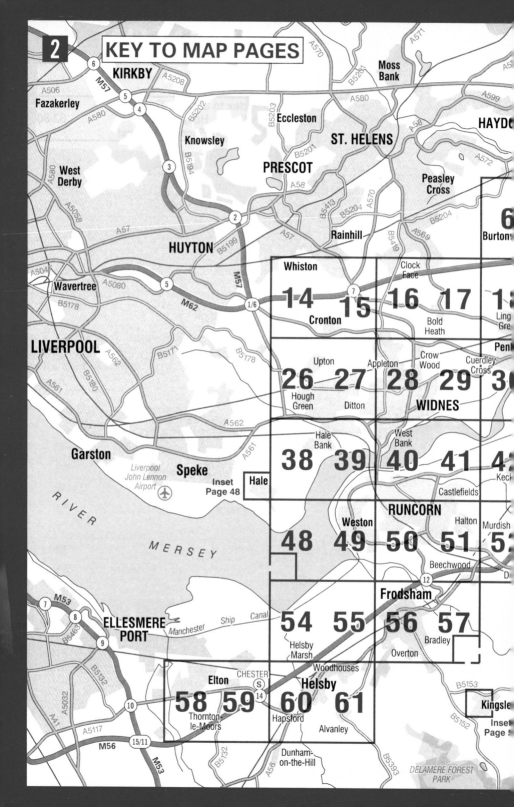

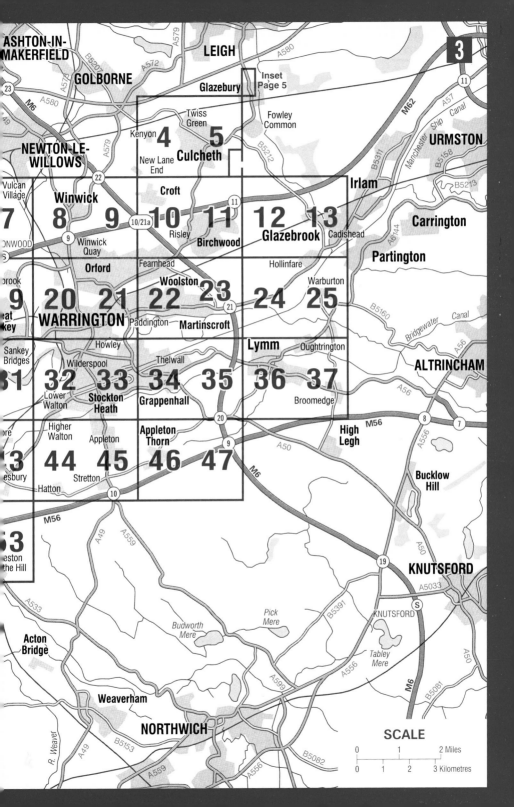

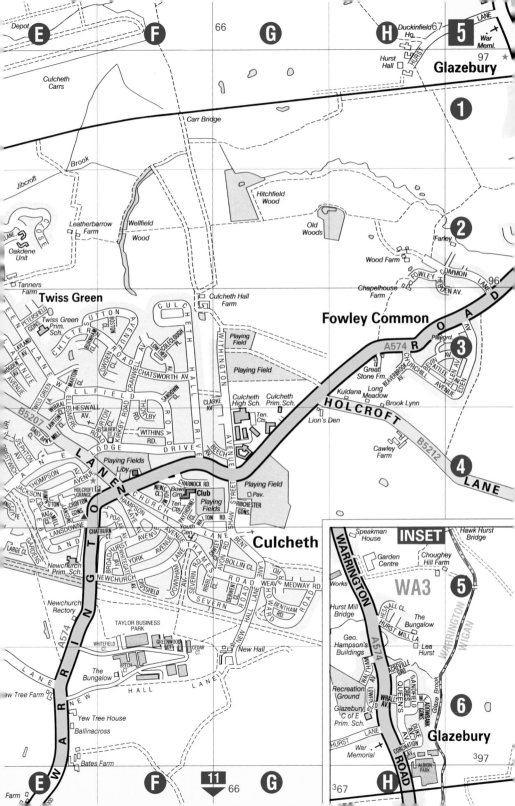

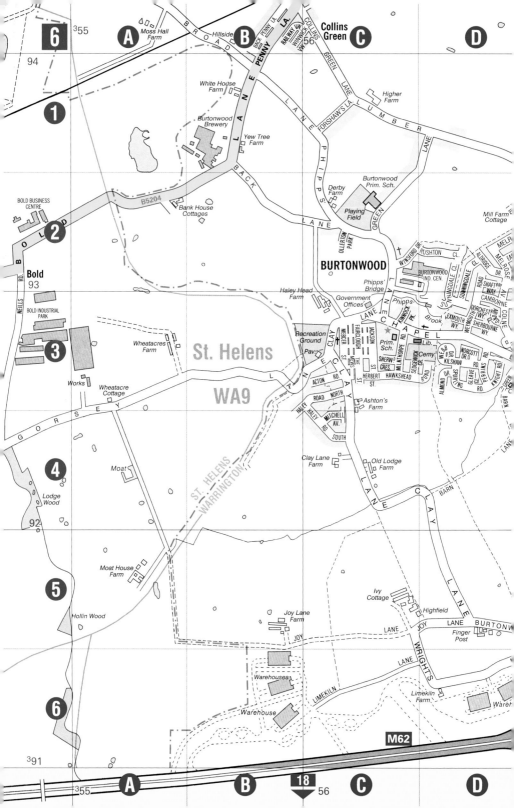

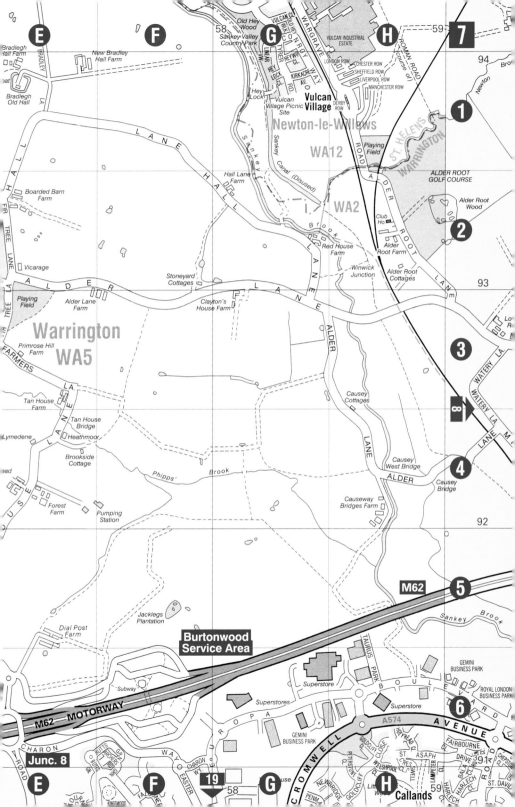

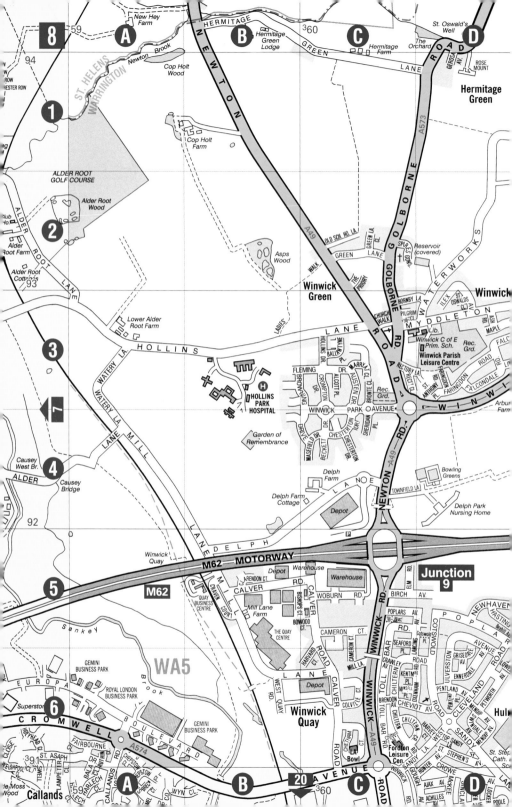

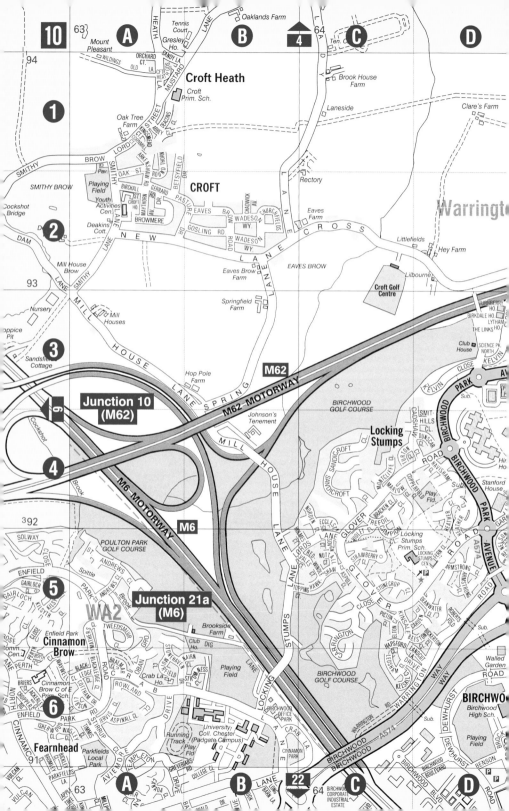

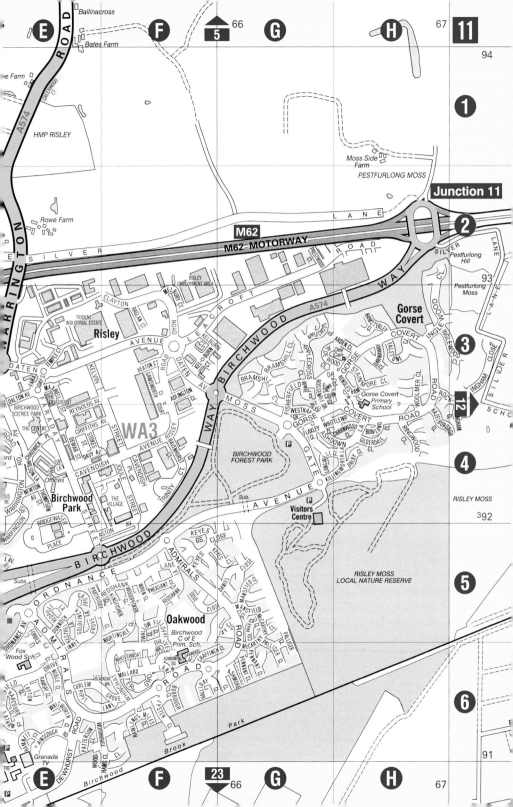

94

A   **B**   **C**   **D**

1

Hole Mill Farm

68 **HOLCROFT**

Alkin Knowles's Bridge

LANE B5212

G L

LONG MOSS

M62

Junction 11

2

M62 MOTORWAY

Nurse

HOLCROFT MOSS

SILVER

Pestfurlong Hill

93

Pestfurlong Moss

LANE

Warrington

3

COVERT

HILSTONE

INGLEWOOD CL.

Gorse Covert

Glazebrook Moss

WA3

Hoyle's Moss Farm

SILVER

CLOSE

ROCKINGHAM

11

WOOLMER CL.

ROCKINGHAM

ROXBOROUGH

SCHOOL

New Hall Farm

LANE

ROAD

RINGWOOD CL.

MOSS

Milverton Farm

D

LANE

4

Omrod Farm

LANE

A

M

Ivy Cottage

RISLEY MOSS

3 92

Bridge Farm

Townley Brow Farm

Hollingreave Farm

RISLEY MOSS LOCAL NATURE RESERVE

5

Moss Hall Farm

6

MOSS SIDE

LANE

Barn End Farm

Ash Tree Farm

Prospect Farm

Moss Side Farm No.2

PROSPECT

LANE

MOSS

91

SIDE

Woodend Farm

24

Moss Side Farm

MOAT LA

Works

67

A   **B**   Woodend Cottage   68   **C**   **D**   RIXTON PARK HOMES

WOODEND

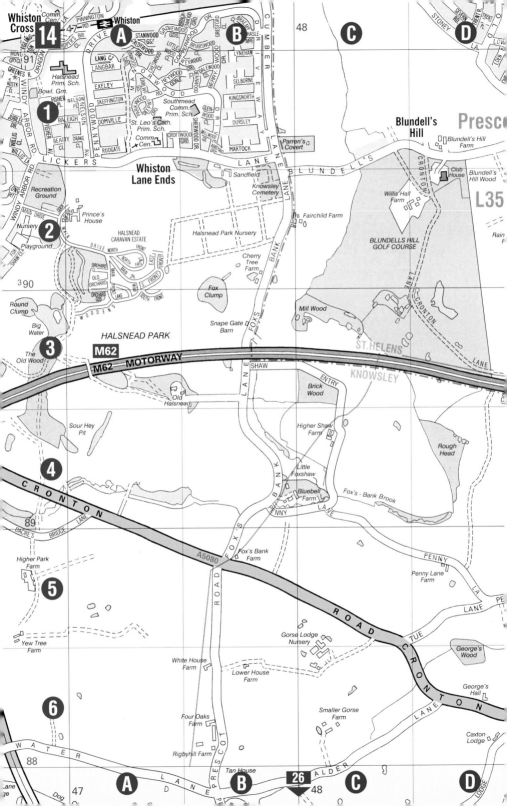

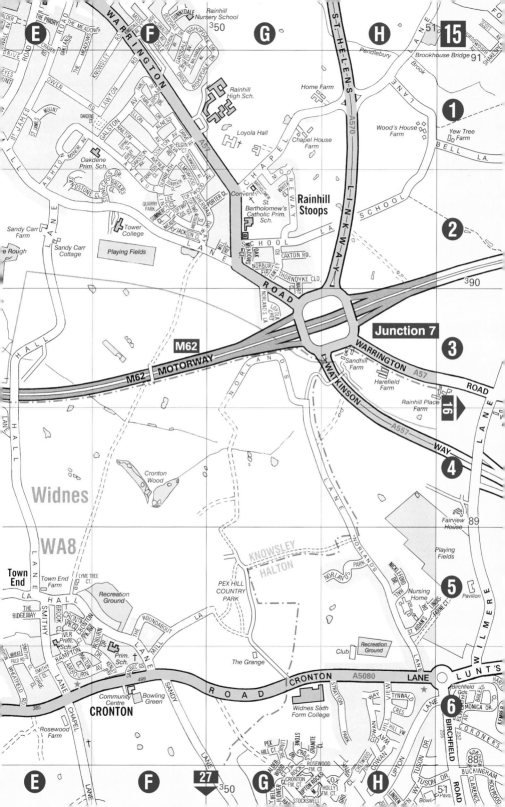

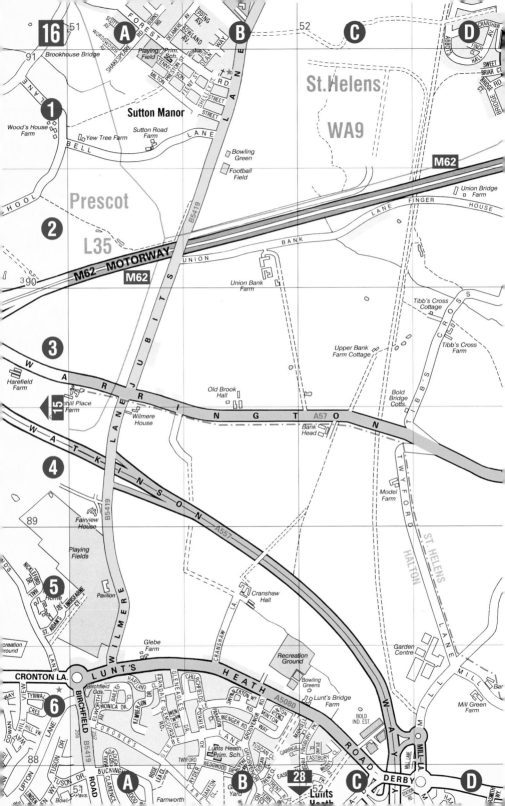

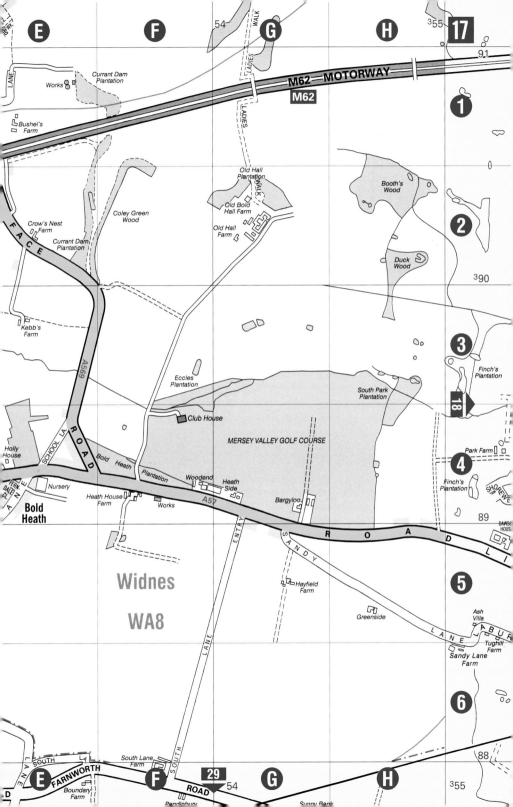

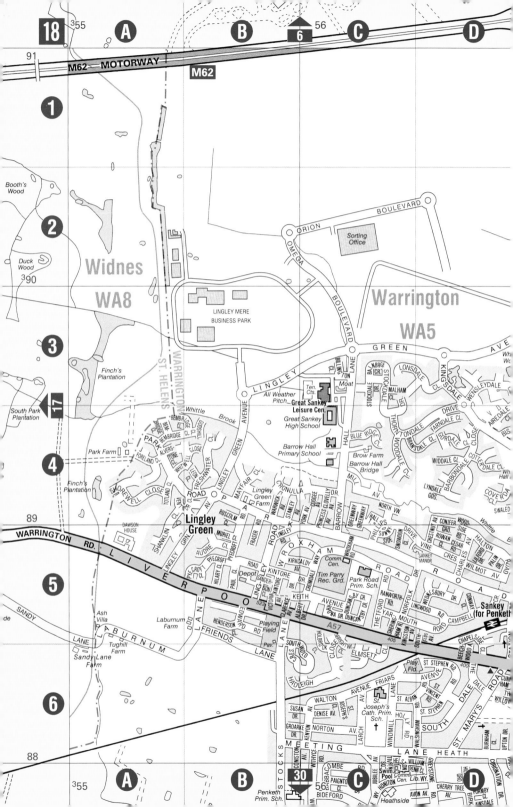

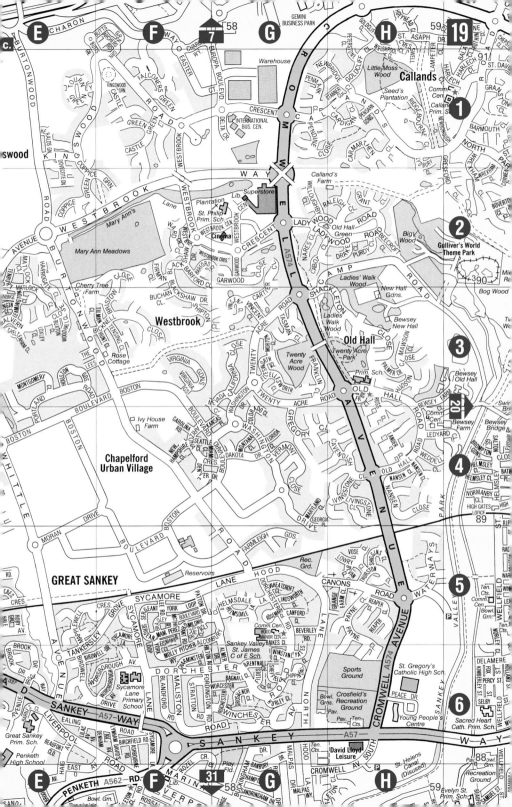

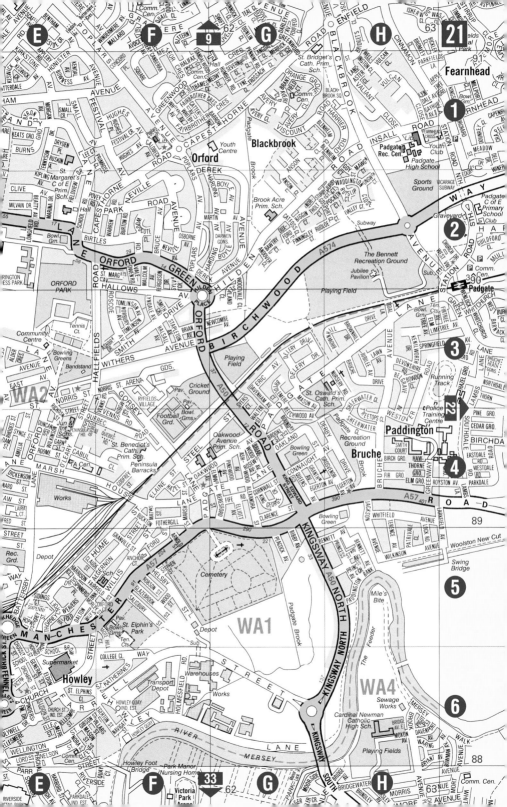

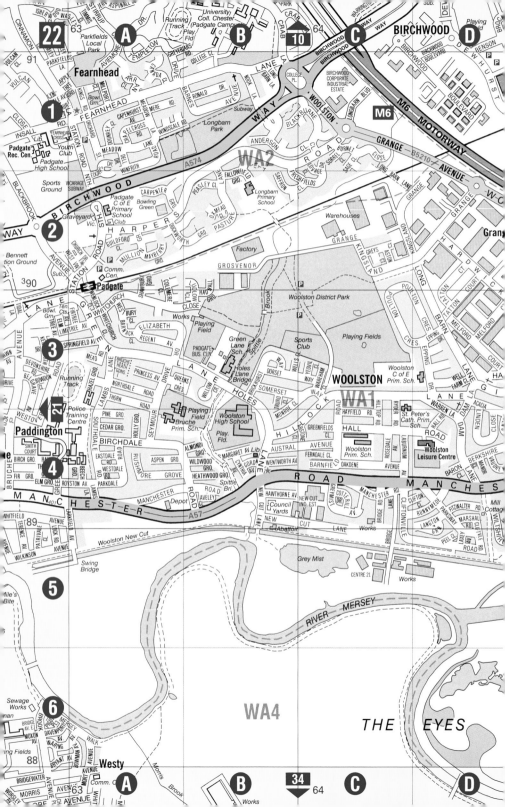

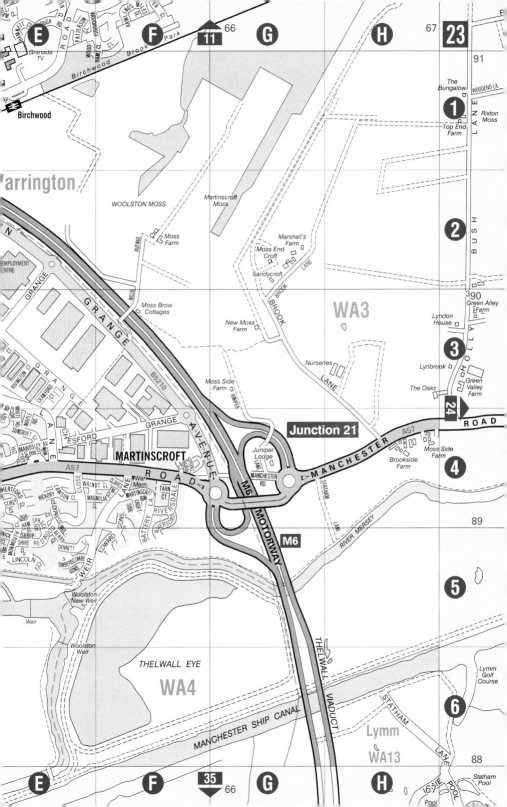

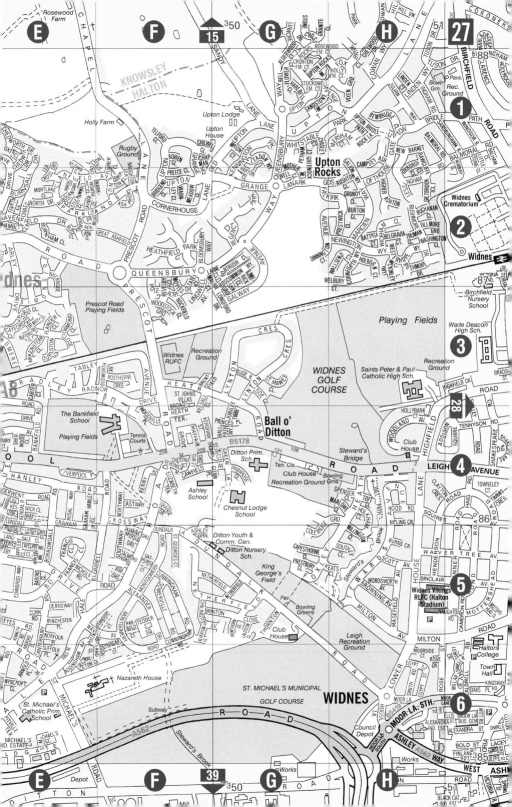

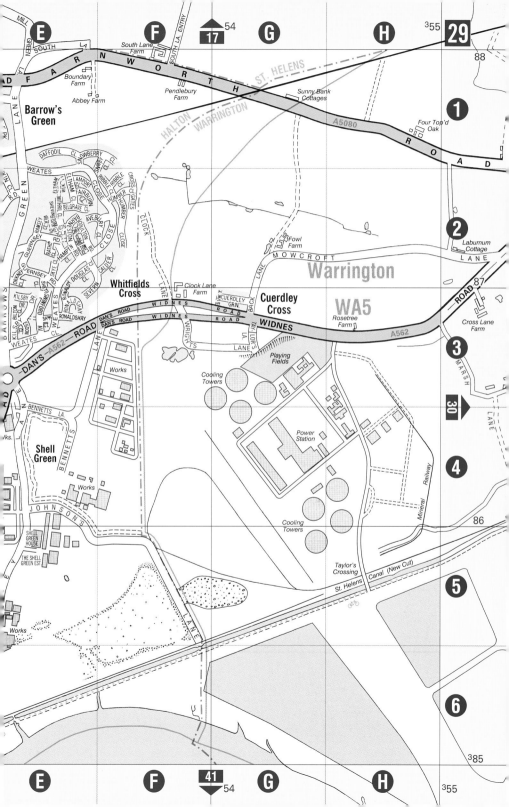

Barrow's
Green

Boundary
Farm

South Lane
Farm

Abbey Farm

Pendlebury
Farm

Sunny Bank
Cottages

Four Top'd
Oak

1

DAFFODIL CL
SNOWBERRY

WEATES

FAIRBURN

CROSS GATES

BELGRAVE CL.

LAMBORT
ELTHAM

MITHRIL CL
SHEVINGTON

RAMSEY

GUERNSEY

ORKNEY GUERNSEY

RONALDSAY DOUGLAS

SEVERN

KILSBY
DR

WEATES

RONALDSHAY

CT.

Fowl
Farm

MOWCROFT   LANE

Warrington

Laburnum
Cottage

2

87

Whitfields
Cross

Clock Lane
Farm

CUERDLEY
GRN.

Cuerdley
Cross

WA5

Rosetree
Farm

Cross Lane
Farm

WIDNES   ROAD

DAN'S A562 ROAD

WIDNES   ROAD

WIDNES

A562

WRIGHTS

TAYLOR'S
LANE

Playing
Fields

3

BENNETTS LA.

Works

Cooling
Towers

30 ▶

MARSH   LANE

Shell
Green

BENNETTS

Works

Power
Station

Railway

4

86

JOHNSONS

SHELL
GREEN
HOUSE

THE SHELL
GREEN EST.

Cooling
Towers

Works

Taylor's
Crossing

St. Helens   Canal (New Cut)

5

6

³85

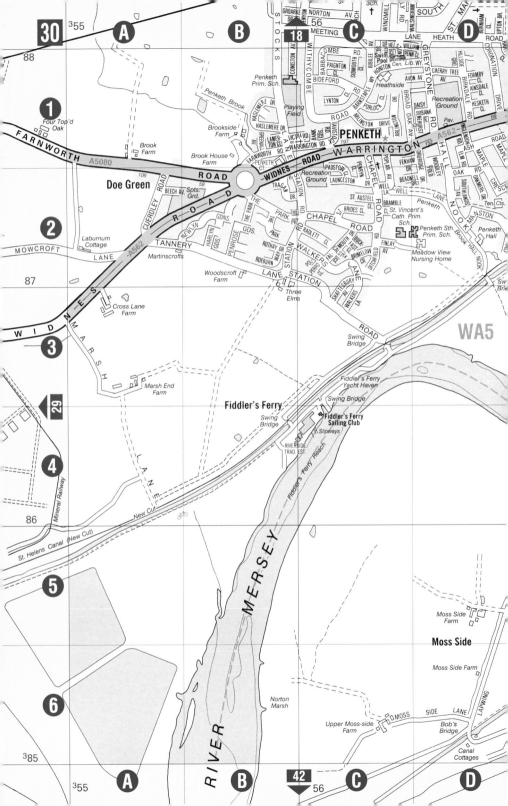

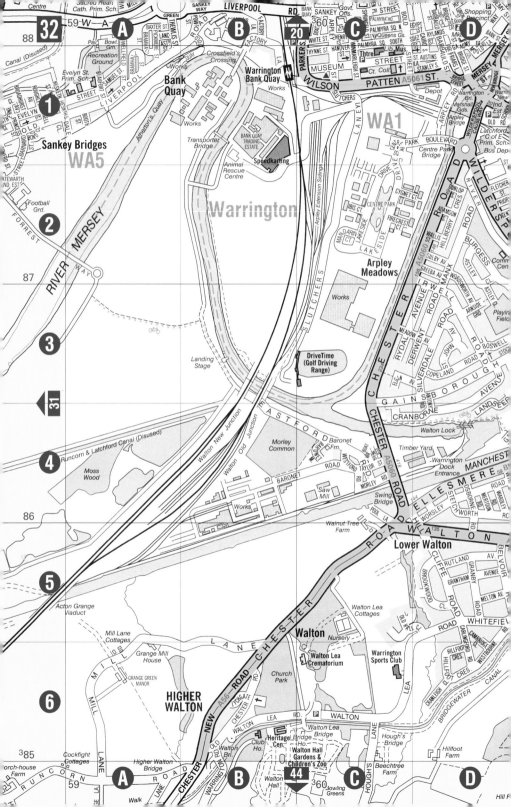

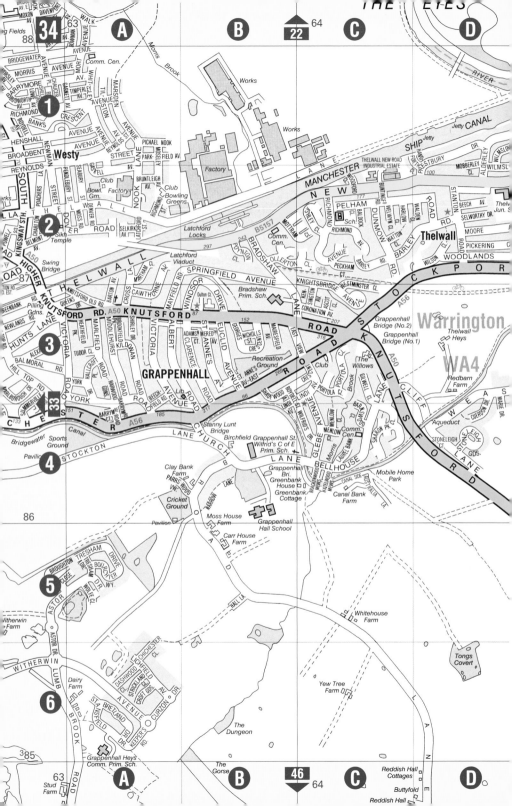

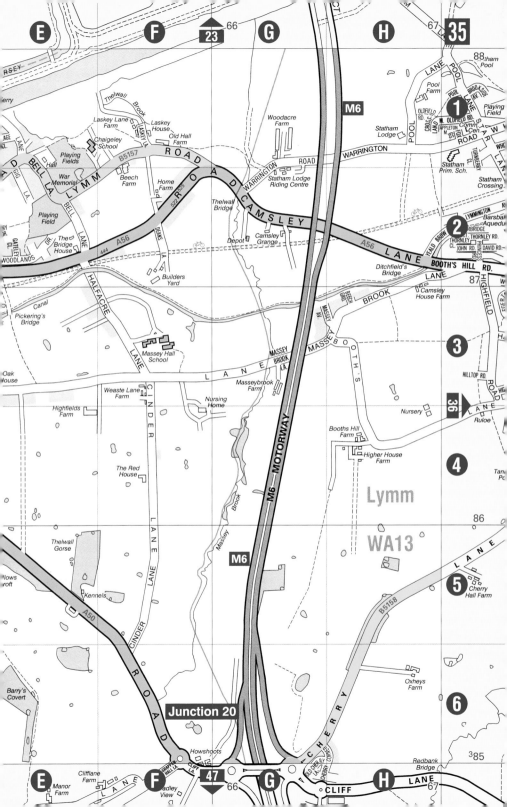

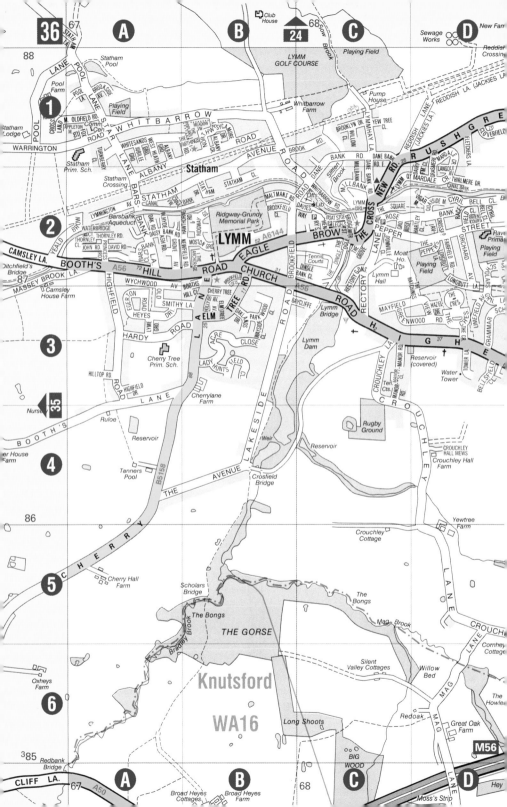

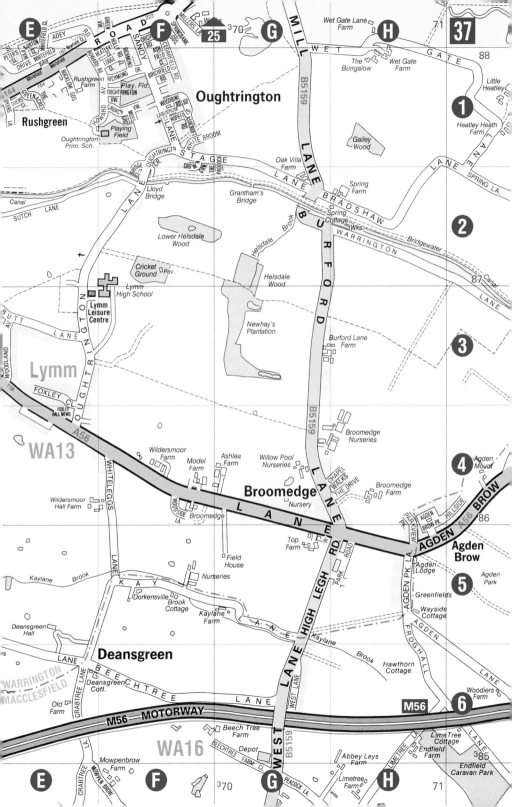

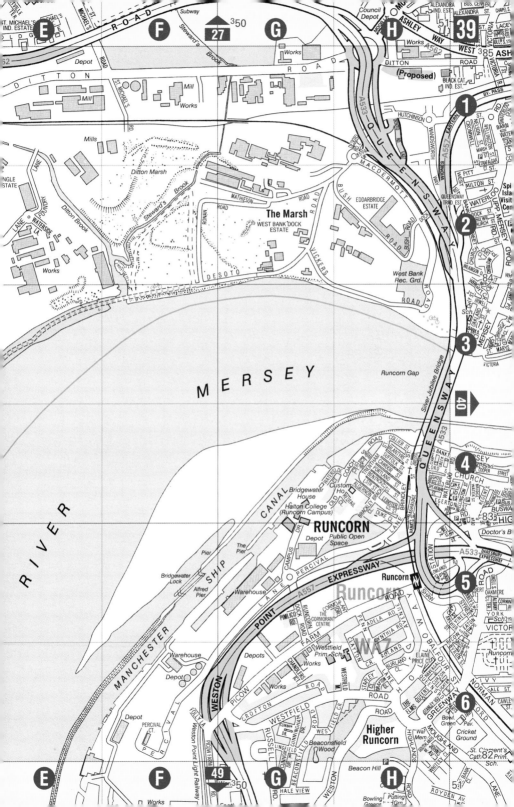

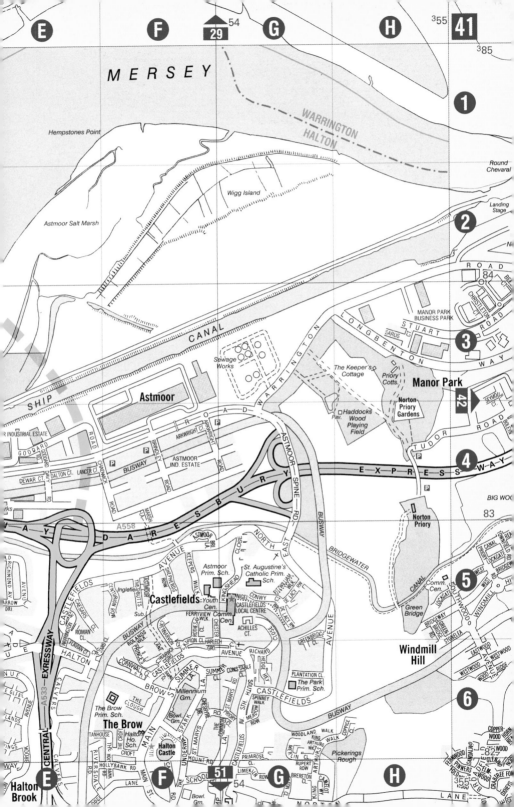

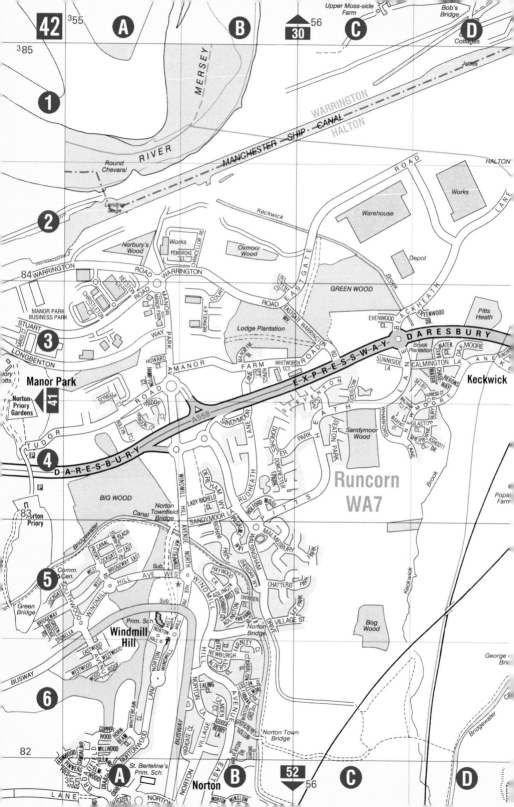

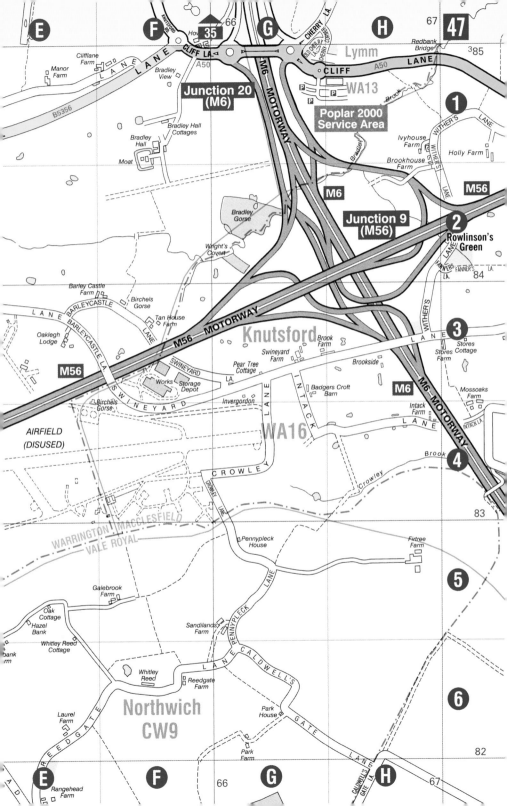

48 47

A WITHIN

B

38 48

C

D

³82

Pav.

Church Willow Bed

Liverpool

L24

END

CHURCH

ROAD

WAY

Willow Bed

Old Pits

1

2

LIGHTHOUSE

81

Lighthouse

Hale Head

3

M E R S E Y

R I V E R

4

³83

RAMSBROOK

Houghton Tower

Liverpool

MORCOTT

LANE

LANE

L24

CARLOW ARKLOW CL

CARR

Brook Farm

LANGFORD

PHEASANT FIELD

LADYPOOL

LANE

WEXFORD CL

MAIN CL

KILDARE CL

AVRIL CT

LANE DR

LANE

HOLLY CL

IVY CL

HALE

HIGH

COCKLADE

PEPPER ST

M & T

CT

TOWN

LANE

Hale

5

Home Farm

ROAD

STREET

War Mem

CHURCH END

CHURCH RD

Old Plantation

6

CARRIAGE DR

Recreation Ground

Bowling Green

Pav.

82

INSET

³46

A

Ice House Plantation

B

Hale Hall

Pool

Lady

47

C

54

D

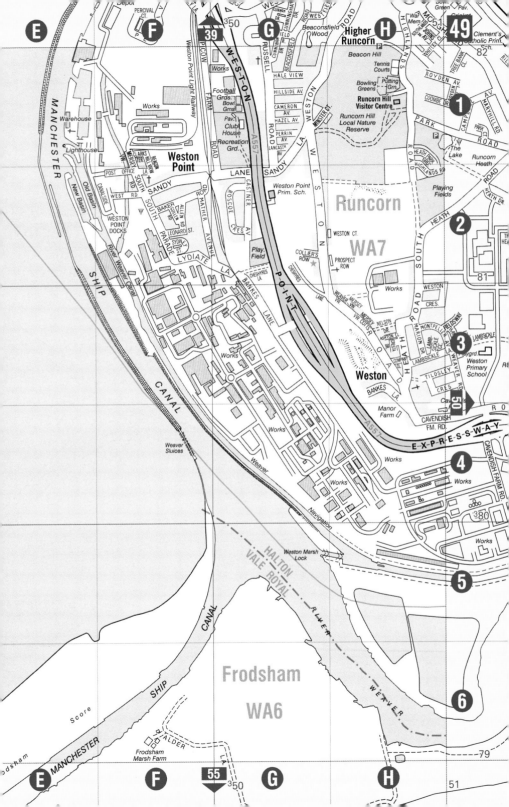

E   **F**   PERCIVAL CT.   **39**   **G**   Beaconsfield Wood   Higher Runcorn   **H**   HIGHLANDS   **49**

War Mem.   St. Clement's Catholic Prim. Sch.   82

WESTON POINT LIGHT RAILWAY   RUSSELL   Beacon Hill   Tennis Courts

Works   HALE VIEW   Bowling Greens   Putting Grn   ROYDEN AV.

Warehouse   Works   Football Grds. Bowl Grns   HILLSIDE AV.   Runcorn Hill Visitor Centre   COOMBE DR.   **1**

CAMERON AV.   HAZEL AV.   Runcorn Hill Local Nature Reserve   PARK   MARYHILL RD.   PARK ROAD

Lighthouse   PERRIN AV.   LANCASTR   The Lake   Runcorn Heath

Weston Point   POST OFFICE   SANDY   LANE   CASTNER   ROP   Weston Point Prim. Sch.   HEATH   HEATH DR.

New Basin   WEST RD.   SOUTH   ROSCOE   **Runcorn**   Playing Fields

WESTON POINT DOCKS   BAKER   ALLEN RD.   CRES.   WESTON CT.   **WA7**   **2**   81

LEONARD ST.   SYDN.   Play Field   COLLIER'S ROW   PROSPECT ROW   SOUTH   WESTON   CRES.

SHIP   LYDIATE LA.   BANKES   WEAVER-MERSEY WV CORNR   Works   HIGH   MONTPELIER AV.   LAMBSICKLE   **3**

River Weaver Canal   CHESHYRES   P-O-I-N-T   NELSON DR.   ASHTONE   COMPANY   LAMBSICKLE   WEAVER RD.   Weston Primary School

Works   BANKES LA.   TILDSLEY CRES.   **Weston**

CANAL   MANCHESTER   Works   Manor Farm   CAVENDISH FM. RD.   **50**   CAVENDISH FARM RD.

Weaver Sluices   Weaver   Navigation   Works   E-X-P-R-E-S-S-W-A-Y   **4**

Works   Works   380

HALTON VALE ROYAL   Weston Marsh Lock   Works   **5**

Score   SHIP   CANAL   **Frodsham**   RIVER   WEAVER   **6**

MANCHESTER   **WA6**

CALDER   Frodsham Marsh Farm   79

odsham   **E**   **F**   **55**   350   **G**   **H**   51

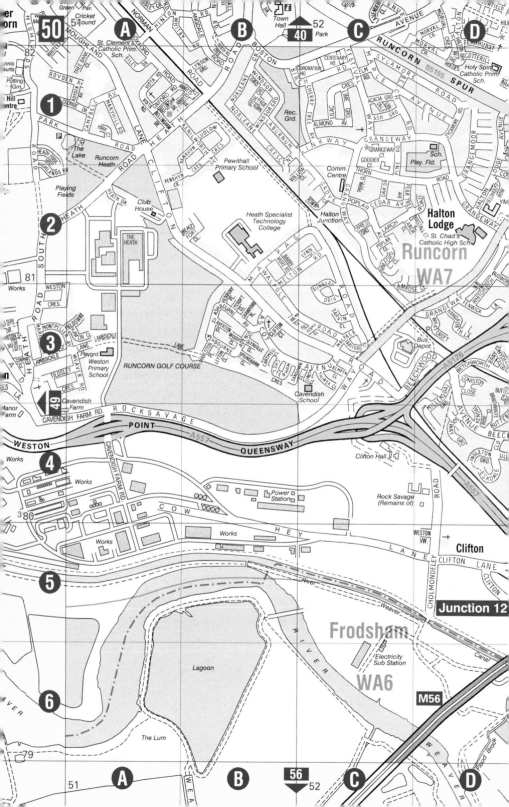

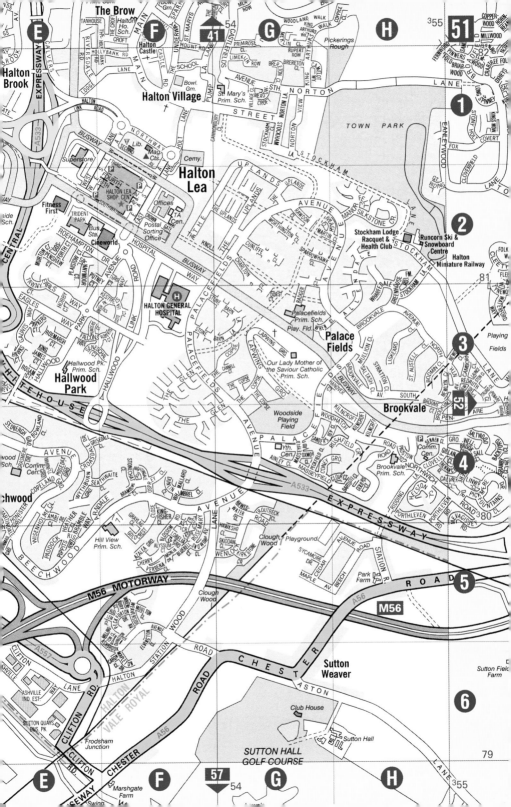

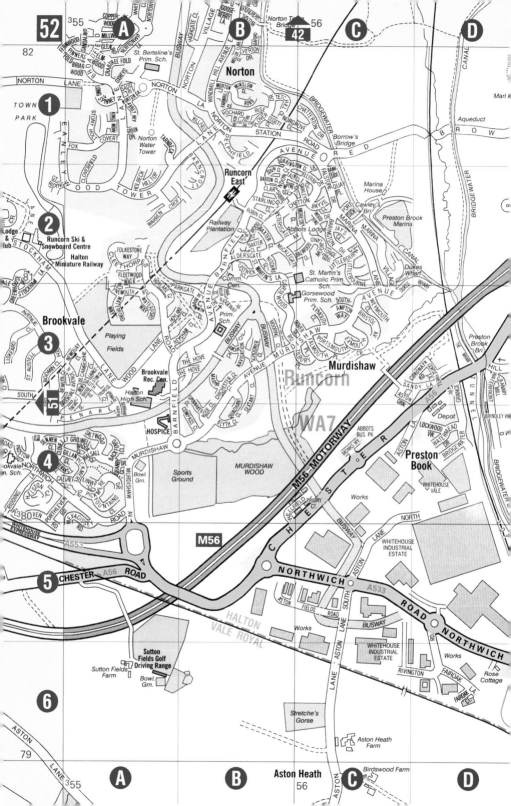

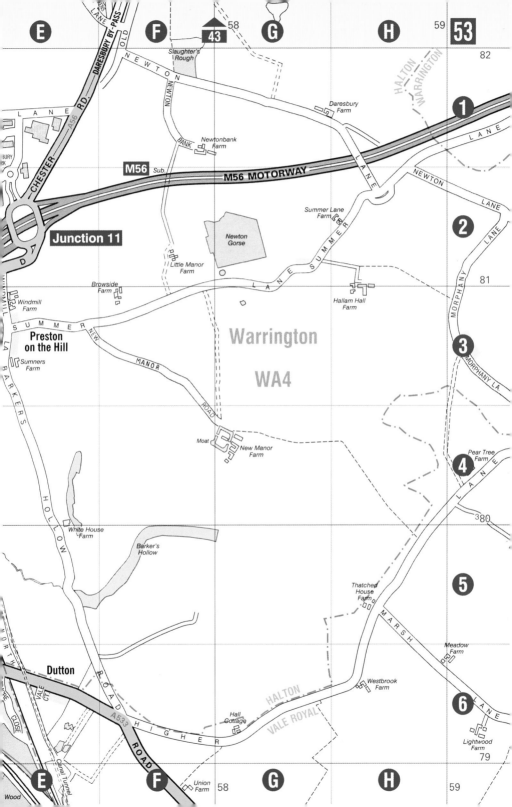

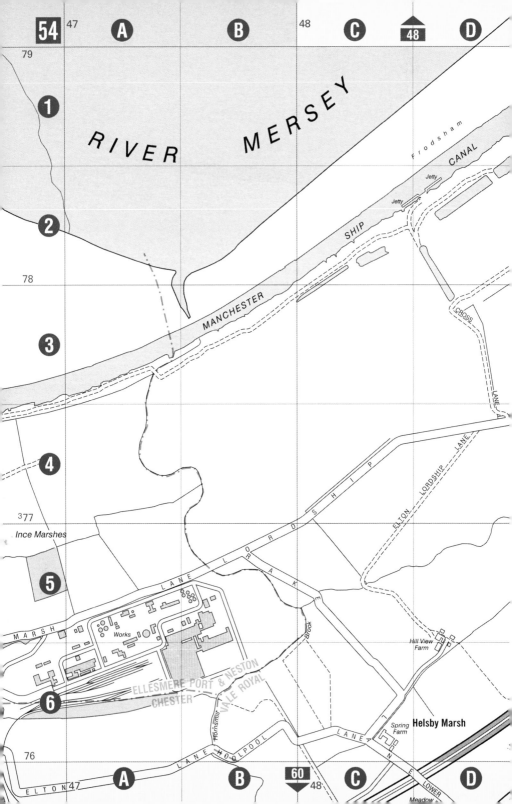

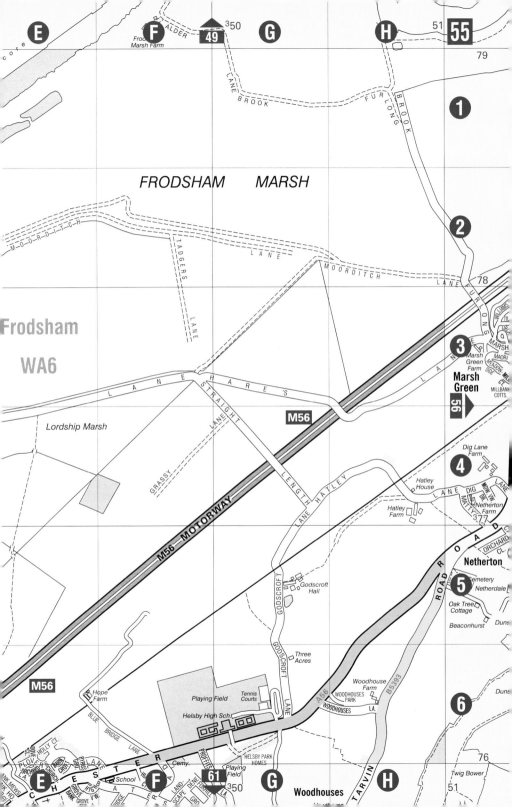

E **F** ALDER **49** 350 **G** **H** 51 **55**

79

Frod
Marsh Farm

LANE
BROOK

FURLONG
BROOK

1

FRODSHAM MARSH

2

78

M-O-O-R-D-I-T-C-H

LANE

MOORDITCH

LANE

FURLONG

TADGERS
LANE

LANE

WILLIAMS
PL.

PUBLIC

Frodsham

WA6

LANE

HARE'S

STRAIGHT

LANE

M56

MARSH
GREEN
MEADOW
SIDE

MAORI
MILL

3

Marsh
Green
Farm

MILLBANK
COTTS.

Marsh
Green

56

Lordship Marsh

GRASSY

LANE

LENGTH

LANE HATLEY

Dig Lane
Farm

4

Hatley
House

LANE DIG
MONTVW.

Netherton
Farm

MATTY

377

M56 MOTORWAY

Hatley
Farm

ORCHARD
CL.

Netherton

Godscroft
Hall

ROAD

Cemetery
Netherdale

5

Oak Tree
Cottage

Duns

Beaconhurst

GODSCROFT

Three
Acres

ROAD

A56

B5393

M56

Hope
Farm

GODSCROFT

LANE

Woodhouse
Farm

WOODHOUSES
PARK

Duns

6

Playing Field

Tennis
Courts

WOODHOUSES

LA.

Helsby High Sch.

BLUE

BRIDGE

LANE

HOLLY CT.

PLOVER
ORCHARD
CROFT

LANE

CROFT
GROVE

CHESTER

Cemy.

PROFITS

LAND
SCAPE DENE
CROFT

HELSBY PARK
HOMES

School

TARVIN

76

Twig Bower

E **F** **61** 350 **G** **H** 51

Playing
Field

Woodhouses

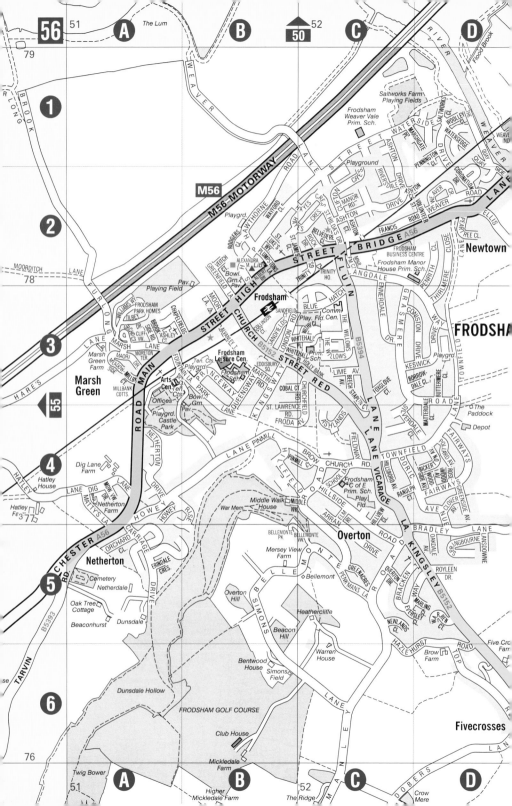

SUTTON QUAYS
BUS. PK.

CLIFTON RD.

Frodsham
Junction

CLIFTON RD.

A557 CHESTER

CAUSEWAY A556

Sutton
Bridge

Marshgate
Farm

Swing
Bridge

Mill Cut

Weaver Navigation (Canal)

River Weaver

51

SUTTON HALL
GOLF COURSE

Lowe's
Wood

Sutton Hall

ASTON LANE

1

Mare
Clough

Kidney
Plantation

Beckett's Wood

Frodsham Lock

Frodsham Cut

ham
ge

Frodsham

WA6

Runcorn

WA7

2

78

Dell Wood

3

Weaver

Blackamoor
Wood

Bradley
Orchard
Farm

Bradley
Orchard
Cottages

Navigation

4

Bradley
Farm

Dingle
Farm

Bradley

Bradley Hall

Beech
Farm

WATERY LANE

Brook
Farm

Beechmill
House

Fort

Top Mill
Cott.

RY

Hatley
Farm

KINGSLEY GRN

B5152

ROAD

Newton Hall

INSET

HOLLOW

Westbrook
Farm Hall

MILL LA

375

B5153

Cemetery

ROAD

CHURCH
VIEW

WESTBROOK

ACRES

SMITH
CR.

GORSE CL.

GORSE LA

CHESTNUT

Prim.
Sch.

Comm.
Cen.

TOWN
WELL

THE BROW

WELL LA

THE

CHAPEL LA.

RODDY
LANE

Sunningdale

LANE

CHAMBER BROOK LA.

HURST

HIGHBANK

ROAD

BROOKSIDE

THE HURST

Playing
Field

Rose
Cottage

Ivy
House

Kingsley

THE LANE

ROAD THE

PLANTERS ROAD

SHELLEYS

HILL VIEW

Frodsham

WA6

5

6

DARK LANE

MANOR RD.

MANS FIELD

BEECH

HIGHER HEYES DR.

Depot

GUEST SLACK

TOP RD.

B5152

355

Beech
Farm

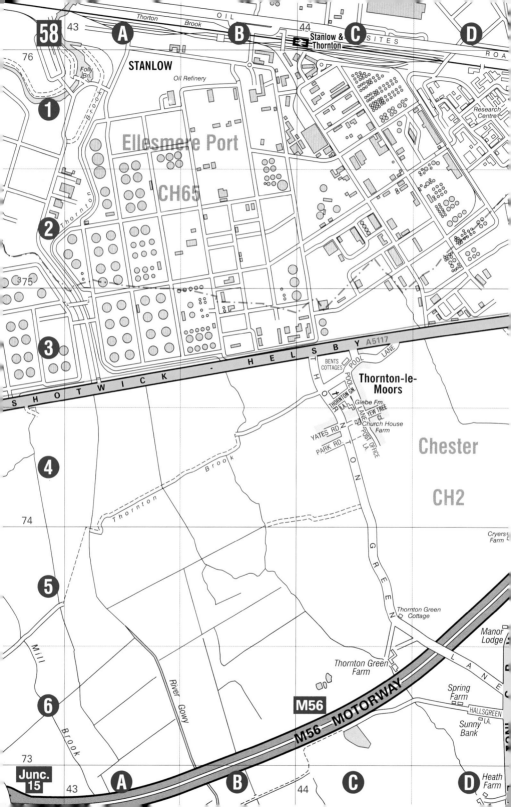

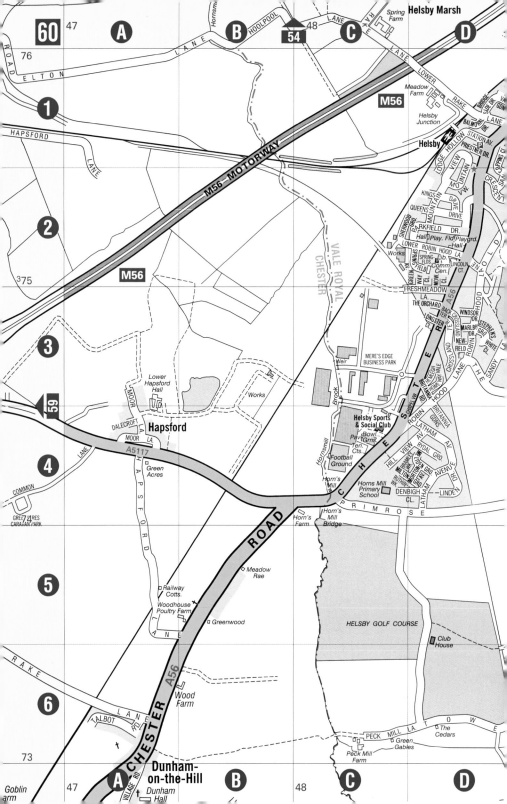

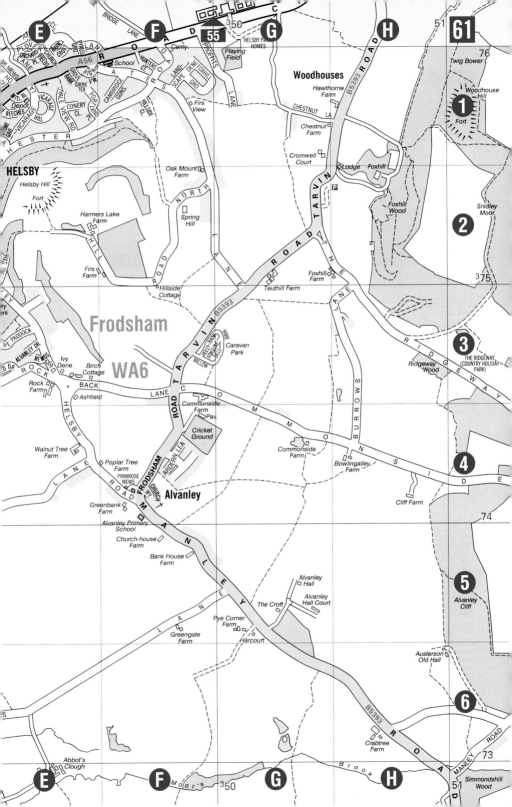

INDEX

Including Streets, Places & Areas, Hospitals & Hospices, Industrial Estates,
Selected Flats & Walkways, Stations, and Selected Places of Interest.

HOW TO USE THIS INDEX

1. Each street name is followed by its Postcode District and then by its Locality abbreviation(s) and then by its map reference;
e.g. **Abbey Rd.** WA8: Wid . . . .5E **27** is in the WA8 Postcode District and the Widnes Locality and is to be found in square 5E on page **27**.
The page number is shown in bold type.

2. A strict alphabetical order is followed in which Av., Rd., St., etc. (though abbreviated) are read in full and as part of the street name;
e.g. **Abbotsfield Cl.** appears after **Abbots Bus. Pk.** but before **Abbots Hall Av.**

3. Streets and a selection of flats and walkways too small to be shown on the maps, appear in the index with the thoroughfare to which it is connected shown in
brackets; e.g. **Bk. Eastford Rd.** WA4: Warr . . . .4C **32** (off Eastford Rd.)

4. Addresses that are in more than one part are referred to as not continuous.

5. Places and areas are shown in the index in BLUE TYPE and the map reference is to the actual map square in which the town centre or area is located and not to the
place name shown on the map; e.g. AGDEN BROW 5H **37**

6. An example of a selected place of interest is Castle Pk. Arts Cen. 3A **56**

7. An example of a station is Birchwood Station (Rail) 1E **23**

8. An example of a hospital is HALTON GENERAL HOSPITAL 3F **51**

GENERAL ABBREVIATIONS

Av. : Avenue	Dr. : Drive	Mans. : Mansions	Sth. : South
Bk. : Back	E. : East	Mkt. : Market	Sq. : Square
Blvd. : Boulevard	Est. : Estate	Mdw. : Meadow	Sta. : Station
Bri. : Bridge	Fld. : Field	Mdws. : Meadows	St. : Street
Bus. : Business	Gdns. : Gardens	M. : Mews	Ter. : Terrace
Cvn. : Caravan	Ga. : Gate	Mt. : Mount	Trad. : Trading
C'way. : Causeway	Gt. : Great	Nth. : North	Up. : Upper
Cen. : Centre	Grn. : Green	Pde. : Parade	Va. : Vale
Cl. : Close	Gro. : Grove	Pk. : Park	Vw. : View
Comn. : Common	Ho. : House	Pl. : Place	Vs. : Villas
Cnr. : Corner	Ind. : Industrial	Prom. : Promenade	Vis. : Visitors
Cotts. : Cottages	Info. : Information	Ri. : Rise	Wlk. : Walk
Ct. : Court	La. : Lane	Rd. : Road	W. : West
Cres. : Crescent	Lwr. : Lower	Rdbt. : Roundabout	Yd. : Yard
Cft. : Croft	Mnr. : Manor	Shop. : Shopping	

LOCALITY ABBREVIATIONS

Alv : **Alvanley**	Dares : **Daresbury**	K'ley : **Kingsley**	Rix : **Rixton**
Ant : **Antrobus**	Dun H : **Dunham-on-the-Hill**	Latch : **Latchford**	Run : **Runcorn**
App : **Appleton**	Dutt : **Dutton**	Lit Stan : **Little Stanney**	Speke : **Speke**
App T : **Appleton Thorn**	Ell P : **Ellesmere Port**	Lwr S : **Lower Stretton**	S Hth : **Stockton Heath**
Arl : **Arley**	Elt : **Elton**	Lwr Wh : **Lower Whitley**	S'ton : **Stretton**
Ast : **Astmoor**	Fearn : **Fearnhead**	Low : **Lowton**	Sut M : **Sutton Manor**
Aston : **Aston**	Frod : **Frodsham**	Lymm : **Lymm**	Sut W : **Sutton Weaver**
Beech : **Beechwood**	G'brk : **Glazebrook**	Manl : **Manley**	Tar G : **Tarbock Green**
Bchwd : **Birchwood**	G'bury : **Glazebury**	Mnr P : **Manor Park**	Thel : **Thelwall**
Bold : **Bold**	Grap : **Grappenhall**	Moore : **Moore**	Thor M : **Thornton-le-Moors**
Bold H : **Bold Heath**	Gt San : **Great Sankey**	Murd : **Murdishaw**	Walt : **Walton**
Brook : **Brookvale**	Hale : **Hale**	New W : **Newton-le-Willows**	Warb : **Warburton**
B'wood : **Burtonwood**	Hale B : **Hale Bank**	Nort : **Norton**	Warr : **Warrington**
Cad : **Cadishead**	Halew : **Halewood**	Old H : **Old Hall**	W'brk : **Westbrook**
Call : **Callands**	Halt : **Halton**	P'ton : **Paddington**	West : **Weston**
Cas : **Castlefields**	Hap : **Hapsford**	P'gate : **Padgate**	West P : **Weston Point**
Cliftn : **Clifton**	Hatt : **Hatton**	Pal F : **Palace Fields**	Westy : **Westy**
Clock F : **Clock Face**	Hel : **Helsby**	Part : **Partington**	Whis : **Whiston**
C Grn : **Collins Green**	H Walt : **Higher Walton**	Penk : **Penketh**	Wid : **Widnes**
Croft : **Croft**	H Legh : **High Legh**	Pres B : **Preston Brook**	Wim T : **Wimbolds Trafford**
Cron : **Cronton**	Hou G : **Houghton Green**	Pres H : **Preston on the Hill**	Wind H : **Windmill Hill**
Cuerd : **Cuerdley**	Ince : **Ince**	R'hill : **Rainhill**	Win : **Winwick**
Cul : **Culcheth**	Irlam : **Irlam**	Ris : **Risley**	W'ston : **Woolston**

A

	Academy St. WA1: Warr 6D 20	Adlington Ct. WA3: Ris 3F 11	Albany Gro. WA13: Lymm 1A 36
	Academy Way WA1: Warr 6D 20	Adlington Rd. WA7: Wind H 5B 42	Albany Rd. WA13: Lymm 2A 36
	Achilles Av. WA2: Warr 1D 20	Admirals Rd. WA3: Bchwd 5E 11	Albany Ter. WA7: Run 5A 40
Abbey Cl. WA3: Croft 1A 10	Achilles Ct. WA7: Cas 5G 41	Admirals Sq. WA3: Bchwd 6F 11	Albert Dr. WA5: Gt San 5B 18
WA8: Wid 5E 27	Ackerley Cl. WA2: Fearn 6H 9	Afton WA8: Wid 3C 26	Albert Rd. WA4: Grap 3A 34
Abbey Hey WA7: Nort 1A 52	Ackers La. WA4: S Hth 3G 33	AGDEN BROW 5H 37	WA8: Wid 5B 28
Abbey Rd. WA8: Wid 5E 27	Ackers Rd. WA4: S Hth 4G 33	Agden Brow WA13: Lymm 5H 37	Albert Row WA6: Frod 2B 56
Abbeywood Gro. L35: Whis 1B 14	Acrefield Rd. WA8: Wid 4D 26	Agden Brow Pk.	Albert Sq. WA8: Wid 5B 28
Abbots Bus. Pk. WA7: Pres B . . .4C 52	Acres Cres. WA6: K'ley 5G 57	WA13: Lymm 4H 37	Albert St. M44: Cad 3H 13
Abbotsfield Cl. WA4: App 1G 45	Acreville Gro. WA3: G'bury 6H 5	Agden La.	WA7: Run 5A 40
Abbots Hall Av. WA9: Clock F . . .1D 16	Acton Av. WA4: App 4F 45	WA13: H Legh, Lymm 5H 37	Albion Pk. WA3: G'bury 6H 5
Abbotts Cl. WA7: Run 1A 50	Acton Rd. WA5: B'wood 3C 6	Agden Pk. La. WA13: Lymm . . .5H 37	Albright Rd. WA8: Wid 1C 38
Aberdare Cl. WA5: Call 2A 20	Adamson Cl. WA4: Grap 3B 34	Ainley Cl. WA7: Brook 4G 51	Albury Cl. WA5: Warr 4B 20
Abingdon Av. WA1: W'ston 4E 23	Adamson St. WA4: Warr 2D 32	Ainscough Rd. WA3: Bchwd . . .6E 11	Alcock St. WA7: Run 4A 40
Abington Wlk. WA7: Brook 4A 52	Adam St. WA2: Warr 4E 21	Ainsdale Cl. WA5: Penk 1D 30	Alconbury Cl.
Abstone Cl. WA1: W'ston 4C 22	Adderley Cl. WA7: Run 6C 40	Aire WA8: Wid 3D 26	WA5: Gt San 5F 19
Acacia Av. WA1: W'ston 3D 22	Addingham Av. WA8: Wid 6E 27	Airedale Cl. WA5: Gt San 4D 18	Alcott Pl. WA2: Warr 3C 8
WA8: Wid 2B 28	Addison Sq. WA8: Wid 4H 27	Ajax Av. WA2: Warr 1D 20	Alder Av. WA8: Wid 2A 28
Acacia Cl. CH2: Elt 2G 59	Adelaide Ct. WA8: Wid 6A 28	Alamein Cres. WA2: Warr 4D 20	Alderbank Rd.
Acacia Gro. WA7: Run 1C 50	Adela Rd. WA7: Run 5H 39	Alban Retail Pk. WA2: Warr . . .1C 20	WA5: Gt San 5E 19
Academy Pl. WA1: Warr 6D 20	Adey Rd. WA13: Lymm 6E 25	Albany Cres. WA13: Lymm 1B 36	Alder Cres. WA2: Warr 3E 21

Alder La. WA2: Warr 3D 20
WA5: B'wood 2E 7
WA6: Frod 6F 49
WA8: Cron 1B 26
Alderley Rd. WA4: Thel 2D 34
Alder Rd. WA1: W'ston 4D 22
Alder Root La. WA2: Win 2H 7
Aldersey Cl. WA7: Wind H 6B 42
Aldersgate Av. WA7: Murd ...2B 52
Alderwood Ct. WA8: Wid 1G 27
Aldewood Cl. WA3: Bchwd ...3G 11
Aldridge Dr. WA5: B'wood 2D 6
Alexander Dr. WA8: Wid 5F 27
Alexander M. WA7: Run 6C 40
Alexandra Ind. Est.
WA8: Wid 6H 27
Alexandra M. WA6: Frod 2B 56
Alexandra Rd. WA4: Grap 3H 33
WA4: S Hth 4F 33
Alexandra St. WA1: Warr 4G 21
WA8: Wid 6A 28
Alforde St. WA8: Wid 1A 40
(Ashley Rd.)
WA8: Wid 6A 28
(Victoria Sq.)
Alfred Cl. WA8: Wid 5B 28
Alfred St. WA8: Wid 5B 28
Algernon St. WA1: Warr 5F 21
WA4: S Hth 4E 33
WA7: Run 4H 39
Alice Ct. WA8: Wid 3A 40
Allcard St. WA5: Warr 4B 20
Allen Av. WA3: Cul 3H 5
Allenby Rd. M44: Cad 5H 13
Allendale WA7: Pal F 3H 51
Allen Rd. WA7: West P 2F 49
Allen St. WA2: Warr 5C 20
Allerton Rd. WA8: Wid 4B 28
Allotment Rd. M44: Cad 3H 13
All Saints Dr. WA4: Thel 2E 35
Allysum Ct. WA7: Beech 5F 51
Almer Dr. WA5: Gt San 6G 19
Almond Av. WA7: Run 1C 50
Almond Dr. WA5: B'wood 3D 6
Almond Gro. WA1: P'ton 4B 22
WA8: Wid 5F 27
Almond Tree Cl. L24: Hale 6A 38
Almond Wlk. M31: Part 6H 13
Alness Dr. L35: R'hill 1F 15
Alt WA8: Wid 3D 26
ALVANLEY 4F 61
Alvanley Dr. WA6: Hel 3E 61
Alvanley Hall WA6: Alv 5G 61
Alvanley Hall Rd. WA6: Alv ...5G 61
Alvanley Rd. WA6: Hel 2D 60
Alvanley Ter. WA6: Frod 3B 56
Alvanley Vw. CH2: Elt 2F 59
Alva Rd. L35: R'hill 1F 15
Alverstone Cl. WA5: Gt San ...4A 18
Alverton Cl. WA8: Wid 5F 27
Amberleigh Cl. WA4: App T ...3B 46
Ambleside Cl. WA7: Beech 4E 51
Ambleside Cres. WA2: Warr ...6E 9
Amelia Cl. WA8: Wid 1B 28
Amelia St. WA2: Warr 4E 21
Anchorage, The
WA13: Lymm 2B 36
Anchor Cl. WA7: Murd 3B 52
Anchor Ct. WA1: Warr 5F 21
Anderson Cl. L35: R'hill 2F 15
WA2: P'gate 1B 22
Andover Cl. WA2: P'gate 2G 21
Andrew Cl. WA8: Wid 5E 27
Annie St. WA2: Warr 5E 21
Ann St. WA7: Run 4B 40
Ann St. W. WA8: Wid 6B 28
Ansdell Rd. WA8: Wid 3B 28
Antony Rd. WA1: Warr 3D 32
Antrim Rd. WA2: Warr 1C 20
Anvil Cl. CH2: Elt 1F 59
Appleby Cl. WA8: Wid 5E 27
Appleby Rd. WA2: Warr 6E 9
WA8: Wid 5E 27
Appleby Wlk. WA8: Wid 5E 27
Applecross Cl. WA3: Bchwd ...3G 11
Appleford Cl. WA4: App 6G 33
APPLETON
Warrington 6G 33
Widnes 3B 28
Appleton Hall Gdns.
WA4: App 2G 45

Appleton M. WA13: Lymm 1A 36
APPLETON PARK 3F 45
Appleton Rd. WA8: Wid 4B 28
Appleton St. WA8: Wid 1B 40
APPLETON THORN 3B 46
Appleton Thorn Trad. Est.
WA4: App T 1D 46
Appleton Village WA4: Wid ...4A 28
Apple Tree Cl. L24: Hale 6A 38
Appletree Gro. WA2: Fearn ..1H 21
Aragon Ct. WA7: Mnr P 4A 42
Aran Cl. L24: Hale 5B 48
Arbury La. WA2: Win 3E 9
Archer Av. WA4: Latch 3G 33
Archers Rd. WA5: W'brk 6F 7
Arden WA8: Wid 3C 26
Arden Cl. WA3: Bchwd 3H 11
Ardern Lea WA6: Alv 4F 61
Arena Gdns. WA2: Warr 3F 21
Arizona Cres. WA5: Gt San ...4F 19
Arkenshaw Rd. WA3: Croft ...1A 10
Arkenstone Cl. WA8: Wid 3E 27
Arklow Dr. L24: Hale 5B 48
Arkwright Cl. WA7: Ast 4F 41
Arkwright Rd. WA7: Ast 4F 41
Arley Av. WA4: S Hth 4F 33
Arley Dr. WA8: Wid 3C 26
Arley Gro. WA13: Lymm 3E 37
Arley Rd. WA4: App T 4E 33
Arlington Dr. WA5: Penk 1C 30
Armour Av. WA2: Warr 1D 20
Armstrong Cl. WA3: Bchwd ...5D 10
Arncliffe Dr. WA5: B'wood 3D 6
Arndale WA7: Beech 4E 51
Arnhem Cres. WA2: Warr 4E 21
Arnold Pl. WA8: Wid 6E 27
Arnold St. WA1: Warr 5F 21
Arnside Gro. WA4: Warr 3D 32
ARPLEY MEADOWS 2D 32
Arpley Rd. WA1: Warr 1D 32
Arpley St. WA1: Warr 6C 20
Arran Cl. WA2: Fearn 1A 22
Arran Dr. WA6: Frod 4C 56
Arthur St. WA2: Warr 5C 20
WA7: Run 5H 39
Arundell Cl. WA5: B'wood 3D 6
Ascot Av. WA7: Run 3B 50
Ascot Cl. WA1: W'ston 4E 23
WA4: Grap 3C 34
Ash Av. M44: Cad 4H 13
Ashberry Dr. WA4: App T 2B 46
Ashbourne Av. WA7: Run 3B 50
Ashbourne Rd. WA5: Gt San ..6F 19
Ashbrook Av. WA7: Sut W 6F 51
Ashbrook Cres. WA2: Warr ...3F 21
Ashbury Cl. WA7: Wind H 5B 42
Ashcroft Rd. WA13: Lymm ...1F 37
Ashdown La. WA3: Bchwd ...4G 11
Asher Ct. WA4: App T 3D 46
Ashfield Cl. WA13: Lymm 1F 37
Ashford Dr. WA4: App T 4G 45
Ashford Way WA8: Wid 4D 28
Ash Gro. WA4: Warr 2F 33
WA7: Run 1C 50
WA8: Wid 5F 27
Ashlands WA6: Frod 4C 56
Ash La. WA4: App 5G 33
WA8: Wid 4A 26
Ashley Cl. L35: R'hill 1F 15
WA4: Grap 3C 34
Ashley Ct. WA4: App 1E 45
WA6: Frod 3A 56
Ashley Grn. WA8: Wid 5F 27
Ashley Rd. WA7: Run 5D 40
Ashley Way WA8: Wid 1A 40
Ashley Way W. WA8: Wid 6H 27
Ashmore Cl. WA3: Bchwd 6G 11
Ash Priors WA8: Wid 2F 27
Ashridge St. WA7: Run 4H 39
Ash Rd. CH2: Elt 2G 59
M31: Part 6H 13
WA2: Win 3D 8
WA3: Rix 1E 25
WA5: Penk 1D 30
WA13: Lymm 2A 36
Ashton Av. L35: R'hill 2E 15
Ashton Cl. WA6: Frod 2C 56
WA7: West 3H 49
Ashton Dr. WA6: Frod 1C 56
Ashton St. WA2: Warr 5D 20

Ashville Ind. Est.
WA7: Sut W 6E 51
Ashville Way WA7: Sut W 6E 51
Ashwood Av. WA1: Warr 4G 21
Ashwood Cl. WA8: Wid 6C 26
Aspen Gro. WA1: P'ton 4A 22
Aspinall Cl. WA2: Fearn 6A 10
Aspull Cl. WA3: Bchwd 5C 10
Assheton Wlk. L24: Hale 5A 38
Aster Cres. WA7: Beech 4F 51
Astley Cl. WA4: Warr 2D 32
WA8: Wid 2E 27
Astley Rd. M44: Irlam 1H 13
ASTMOOR 4F 41
Astmoor Bri. La. WA7: Cas ...5F 41
Astmoor Ind. Est. WA7: Ast ..4H 41
(Brindley Rd.)
WA7: Ast 4F 41
(Goddard Rd.)
Astmoor La. WA7: Ast 4C 40
WA7: Cas 5F 41
Astmoor Rd. WA7: Ast 4C 40
Astmoor Spine Rd.
WA7: Ast 4G 41
Aston Av. WA3: Ris 5F 11
Aston Ct. WA1: W'ston 2C 22
Aston Fields Rd.
WA7: Pres B 5B 52
Aston Grn. WA7: Pres B 3C 52
ASTON HEATH 6B 52
Aston La. WA7: Pres B 4C 52
WA7: Pres B ....6G 51 & 6C 52
Aston La. Nth. WA7: Pres B ..5C 52
Aston La. Sth. WA7: Pres B ...6C 52
Astor Dr. WA4: Grap 5H 33
Atherton La. M44: Cad 4H 13
Athlone Rd. WA2: Warr 2C 20
Atterbury Cl. WA8: Wid 3E 27
Attlee Av. WA3: Cul 3H 5
Auburn Cl. WA8: Wid 2E 27
Audlem Cl. WA7: Sut W 5F 51
Audre Cl. WA5: Gt San 5B 18
Austen Dr. WA2: Win 3C 8
Austral Av. WA1: W'ston 4B 22
Australia La. WA4: Grap 4C 34
Avebury Cl. WA8: Wid 2E 29
Avocet Cl. WA7: Beech 6F 9
Avon WA8: Wid 3C 26
Avon Av. WA5: Penk 1C 30
Avondale Dr. WA8: Wid 4D 26
Avon Rd. WA3: Cul 5G 5
Aycliffe Wlk. WA8: Wid 5E 27
Aylsham Cl. WA8: Wid 1E 27
Azalea Gro. WA7: Beech 5F 51

B

Babbacombe Rd. WA5: Penk ...1C 30
Bk. Brook Pl. WA4: Westy 2G 33
Bk. Crossland Ter. WA6: Hel ...3D 60
Bk. Eastford Rd. WA4: Warr ...4C 32
(off Eastford Rd.)
Backford Cl. WA7: Brook 4A 52
Bk. High St. WA7: Run 4A 40
Bk. Kerfoot St. WA2: Warr 4C 20
Back La. WA5: C Grn 2B 6
WA5: Cuerd 3G 29
WA6: Alv 3E 61
Bk. Penny La. WA5: C Grn 1B 6
Badger Cl. WA7: Pal F 3G 51
Bagnall Cl. WA5: Gt San 6G 19
Bagot Av. WA5: Warr 3B 20
Baguley Av. WA8: Hale B 2C 38
Baileys Cl. WA8: Wid 6A 16
Bainbridge Cres.
WA5: Gt San 3C 18
Baker St. WA7: West P 2F 49
Bakewell Rd. WA5: B'wood ...2E 7
Bala Cl. WA5: Call 1A 20
Baldock Cl. WA4: Thel 2C 34
Balfour St. WA7: Run 6H 39
Balham Cl. WA8: Wid 1A 28
Ballantyne Pl. WA2: Win 3C 8
Ballater Dr. WA2: Warr 5G 9
Ball Path WA8: Wid 4H 27
Ball Path Way WA8: Wid 4G 27
Balmoral Dr. WA6: Hel 1D 60

Balmoral Rd. WA4: Grap 3H 33
WA8: Wid 1H 27
Bamford Cl. WA7: Run 2C 50
Banbury Dr. WA5: Gt San 1G 31
Bancroft Rd. WA8: Wid 3D 28
Bandon Cl. L24: Hale 5B 48
Bankes La. WA7: West P 3G 49
(not continuous)
Bankfield Av. M44: Cad 4H 13
Bankfield Rd. WA8: Wid 4D 26
Bank Gdns. WA5: Penk 1C 30
Bank Hall Pk. WA7: Hale 1E 33
Bank Ho. La. WA6: Hel 1E 61
Banklands Cl. M44: Cad 4H 13
Bank M. WA6: Hel 1E 61
BANK QUAY 1A 32
Bank Quay Rd. WA1: Warr 6C 20
Bank Quay Trad. Est.
WA1: Warr 1B 32
Banks Cres. WA4: Westy 1H 33
Bankside WA7: Murd 2C 52
Bank St. WA1: Warr 6D 20
(Academy Way)
WA1: Warr 6D 20
(Horrocks La.)
WA3: G'brk 4E 13
WA8: Wid 3A 40
Barbauld St. WA1: Warr 6D 20
Barbondale Cl. WA5: Gt San ...4D 18
Bardsley Av. WA5: Warr 1B 20
Barford Cl. WA5: W'brk 2F 19
Barham Ct. WA3: Ris 5D 10
Barington Dr. WA7: Murd 2C 52
Barker's Hollow Rd.
WA4: Dutt, Pres H 3E 53
Barkin Cen., The WA8: Wid ...5C 28
Barley Castle Cl. WA4: App T ..4B 46
Barleycastle La. WA4: App T ..2D 46
Barleycastle Trad. Est.
WA4: App T 3D 46
Barley Rd. WA4: Thel 2C 34
Barmouth Cl. WA5: Call 1A 20
Barnack Cl. WA1: P'gate 3A 22
Barnard St. WA1: Warr 2H 31
Barn Cft. WA6: Hel 1E 61
Barncroft Rd. WA7: Nort 1H 52
Barnes Av. WA2: Fearn 1B 22
Barnes Cl. WA5: Gt San 6E 19
WA8: Wid 3D 28
Barnes Rd. WA8: Wid 3C 28
Barneston Rd. WA8: Wid 2E 29
Barnfield Av. WA7: Murd 4A 52
Barnfield Rd. WA1: W'ston ...4C 22
Barn La. WA5: B'wood 3D 6
Barnstaple Way WA5: Penk ...1C 30
Barn St. WA8: Wid 1A 40
Barnswood Cl. WA4: Grap 4C 34
Barnwell Av. WA3: Cul 3D 4
Baron Cl. WA1: W'ston 4D 22
Baronet M. WA4: Warr 4C 32
Baronet Rd. WA4: Warr 4C 32
Barons Cl. WA7: Cas 6F 41
WA8: Wid 5E 27
Barrow Av. WA2: Warr 1G 21
Barrow Hall La. WA5: Gt San ..4C 18
BARROW'S GREEN 1D 28
Barrows Grn. La. WA8: Wid ...3E 29
Barrow's Row WA8: Wid 1B 28
Barrule Cl. WA4: App 6F 33
Barrymore Av. WA4: Westy ...1H 33
Barrymore Ct. WA4: Grap 3A 34
Barrymore Rd. WA4: Grap 4A 34
WA7: Run 2B 50
Barry St. WA4: Warr 1E 33
Barsbank Cl. WA13: Lymm ...2A 36
Barsbank La. WA13: Lymm ...2A 36
Barshaw Gdns. WA4: App 4G 45
Bartholomew Cl. L35: R'hill ...2G 15
Bartlegate Cl. WA7: Brook ...4H 51
Barton Av. WA4: Grap 3A 34
Barton Cl. WA7: Murd 2B 52
Bates La. WA6: Hel 1E 61
Batherton Cl. WA8: Wid 6B 28
Bath St. WA1: Warr 6C 20
Battersby La. WA2: Warr 5E 21
Battersea Ct. WA8: Wid 2H 27
Battery La. WA1: W'ston 5F 23
Bawtry Ct. WA2: P'gate 2G 21
Baxter Cl. WA7: Murd 2C 52
(not continuous)
Baxter St. WA5: Warr 6A 20
Baycliffe WA13: Lymm 3C 36
Baycliffe Cl. WA7: Beech 4D 50

Bayswater Cl.—Brindley St.

Bayswater Cl. WA7: Nort ... 3D 42
Bayvil Cl. WA7: Murd ... 2C 52
Beacon Hill Vw. WA7: West P ... 1F 49
Beaconsfield Cres.
WA8: Wid ... 1A 28
Beaconsfield Gro. WA8: Wid ... 1B 28
Beaconsfield Rd. WA7: Run ... 1G 49
WA8: Wid ... 2B 28
Beadnell Dr. WA5: Penk ... 2C 30
Beamish Cl. WA4: App ... 4F 45
Beamont St. WA8: Wid ... 3A 40
Beatrice St. WA4: Warr ... 2F 33
Beatty Av. WA2: Warr ... 2E 21
Beatty Cl. L35: Whis ... 1A 14
Beaufort Cl. WA5: Gt San ... 6E 19
WA7: Run ... 2B 50
WA8: Wid ... 5C 26
Beaufort St. WA5: Warr ... 1A 32
Beaverbrook Av. WA3: Cul ... 3H 5
Bechers WA8: Wid ... 2D 26
Beckenham Cl. WA8: Wid ... 1D 28
Beckett Dr. WA2: Win ... 4C 8
WA13: Warb ... 3F 25
Bedford Gro. M44: Cad ... 3F 13
Bedford St. WA4: S Hth ... 5E 33
Beech Av. WA3: Cul ... 4G 5
WA3: Low ... 1A 4
WA4: Thel ... 2D 34
WA5: Penk ... 2A 30
WA6: Frod ... 3C 56
Beech Ct. WA3: Ris ... 6F 5
Beeches, The WA6: Hel ... 1E 61
Beechfield Rd. WA4: Grap ... 3A 34
Beech Gro. WA1: P'ton ... 4A 22
WA4: Warr ... 2F 33
WA13: Lymm ... 3H 35
Beechmill Dr. WA3: Cul ... 4D 4
Beechmore WA4: Moore ... 2F 43
Beech Rd. WA4: S Hth ... 5E 33
WA7: Run ... 1C 50
WA7: Sut W ... 5H 51
Beech Ter. WA8: Wid ... 3A 40
Beechtree Farm Cl.
WA16: H Legh ... 6G 37
Beechtree La. WA13: Lymm ... 6F 37
Beech Vw. Rd. WA6: K'ley ... 6G 57
Beechways WA4: App ... 1F 45
BEECHWOOD ... 4E 51
Beechwood Av. WA1: P'gate ... 4G 21
WA5: Gt San ... 6D 18
WA7: Beech ... 3C 50
Beechwood La. WA3: Cul ... 3D 4
Beecroft Cl. WA5: Old H ... 2H 19
Beeston Cl. WA3: Bchwd ... 5D 10
Beeston Ct. WA7: Mnr P ... 3A 42
Belgrave Av. WA1: P'gate ... 3H 21
Belgrave Cl. WA8: Wid ... 2E 29
Belgrave Rd. M44: Cad ... 4H 13
Belgravia Ct. WA8: Wid ... 2H 27
Bellcast Cl. WA4: App ... 2E 45
Bellemonte Pk. WA6: Frod ... 5B 56
Bellemonte Rd. WA6: Frod ... 5B 56
Bellemonte Vw. WA6: Frod ... 5C 56
Bellflower Cl. WA8: Wid ... 1G 27
Bellhouse La. WA4: Grap ... 4C 34
WA4: H Walt ... 6H 31
Bell Ho. Rd. WA8: Wid ... 4C 28
Bellingham Dr. WA7: Run ... 1A 50
Bell La. L35: R'hill ... 1A 16
WA4: Thel ... 2E 35
WA9: Sut M ... 1A 16
Bellsfield Cl. WA13: Lymm ... 3D 36
Belmont Av. WA4: Westy ... 2H 33
Belmont Cres. WA5: Gt San ... 5D 18
Belmont Rd. WA8: Wid ... 3D 28
Belvedere Cl. WA6: Frod ... 2C 56
Belvoir Rd. WA4: Walt ... 5D 32
WA8: Wid ... 4B 28
Bembridge Cl. WA5: Gt San ... 4A 18
WA8: Wid ... 1H 27
Bennett Av. WA1: Warr ... 5G 21
Bennetts La. WA8: Wid ... 4E 29
Bennett St. WA1: Warr ... 6D 20
Benson Rd. WA3: Bchwd ... 6D 10
Bentham Av. WA2: Warr ... 6E 9
Bentham Rd. WA3: Cul ... 5G 5
Bentinck St. WA7: Run ... 4H 39
Bent La. WA3: Cul ... 5G 5
WA13: Warb ... 5G 25
Bents Cotts. CH2: Thor M ... 3C 58
Beresford St. WA1: Warr ... 4G 21
Berkeley Cl. WA5: Warr ... 5B 20
Berkeley Ct. WA7: Mnr P ... 3B 42
Berkshire Dr. M44: Cad ... 4G 13
WA1: W'ston ... 4D 22
Bermondsey Gro. WA8: Wid ... 1D 28
Bernard Av. WA4: App ... 5F 33
Berry Rd. WA8: Wid ... 4F 27
Berrywood Dr. L35: Whis ... 1B 14
Berwick Cl. WA1: W'ston ... 5E 23
Betchworth Cres.
WA7: Beech ... 3D 50
Betjeman Cl. WA4: Westy ... 1H 33
Betsyfield Dr. WA3: Croft ... 2A 10
Bevan Cl. WA5: Gt San ... 5H 19
Beverley Av. WA4: App ... 5F 33
Beverley Rd. WA5: Gt San ... 5G 19
Bevin Av. WA3: Cul ... 3H 5
Bewsey Bus. Cen.
WA5: Warr ... 5B 20
Bewsey Farm Cl. WA5: Old H ... 3H 19
Bewsey Ind. Est. WA5: Warr ... 4C 20
Bewsey Pk. Cl. WA5: Warr ... 4B 20
Bewsey Rd. WA2: Warr ... 4B 20
WA5: Warr ... 4B 20
Bewsey Rd. Bus. Cen.
WA5: Warr ... 4B 20
Bewsey St. WA2: Warr ... 5C 20
(not continuous)
Bexhill Av. WA2: Warr ... 5D 8
(not continuous)
Bibby Av. WA1: Warr ... 5G 21
Bickerton Av. WA6: Frod ... 4D 56
Bickerton Cl. WA3: Bchwd ... 5D 10
Bickley Cl. WA2: Fearn ... 6H 9
WA7: Run ... 6C 40
Bicknell Cl. WA5: Gt San ... 3F 19
Bideford Rd. WA5: Penk ... 1C 30
Biggin Ct. WA2: P'gate ... 2G 21
Billington Cl. WA5: Gt San ... 3C 18
Billington Rd. WA8: Wid ... 2D 26
Bilton Cl. WA8: Wid ... 3E 29
Birchall Av. WA3: Cul ... 3D 4
Birchall St. WA3: Croft ... 2A 10
Birch Av. M44: Cad ... 4H 13
WA2: Win ... 5C 8
Birch Brook Rd.
WA13: Lymm ... 6F 25
Birchdale Cres. WA4: App ... 5E 33
Birchdale Rd. WA1: P'ton ... 4A 22
WA4: App ... 6E 33
Birchfield Av. WA8: Wid ... 3A 28
Birchfield Rd. WA5: Gt San ... 6F 19
WA8: Wid ... 6A 16
WA13: Lymm ... 1F 37
Birch Gro. WA1: P'ton ... 4H 21
WA4: Warr ... 2F 33
Birch Rd. M31: Part ... 6H 13
WA3: Rix ... 6F 13
WA7: Run ... 1B 50
WA8: Wid ... 2B 28
Birchways WA4: App ... 2G 45
Birchwood Blvd.
WA3: Bchwd ... 6C 10
Birchwood Cl. CH2: Elt ... 2G 59
Birchwood Corporate Ind. Est.
WA2: Bchwd ... 1C 22
Birchwood La. WA4: Moore ... 5F 31
Birchwood Leisure and
Tennis Complex ... 6E 11
Birchwood Office Pk.
WA2: Fearn ... 6B 10
BIRCHWOOD PARK ... 4E 11
Birchwood Pk. Av.
WA3: Bchwd, Ris ... 4D 10
Birchwood Science Pk.
WA3: Ris ... 4E 11
Birchwood Shop. Cen.
WA3: Bchwd ... 1D 22
Birchwood Station (Rail) ... 1E 23
Birchwood Way WA2: P'gate ... 3G 21
WA3: Bchwd ... 6C 10
Birdwell Dr. WA5: Gt San ... 6E 19
Birkdale Ho. WA3: Ris ... 3D 10
Birkdale Rd. WA5: Penk ... 1D 30
WA8: Wid ... 6B 16
Birnam Dr. L35: R'hill ... 1F 15
Birstall Ct. WA7: Run ... 2D 50
Birtles Rd. WA2: Warr ... 2E 21
Birtley Ct. WA8: Wid ... 3D 26
Bisham Pk. WA7: Nort ... 5B 42
Bishopdale Cl. WA5: Gt San ... 4D 18
Bishopdale Dr. L35: R'hill ... 1F 15
Bishops Ct. WA2: Win ... 5B 8
Bishops Way WA8: Wid ... 2D 28
Bispham Rd. WA5: Gt San ... 1F 31
Bittern Cl. WA2: Warr ... 6F 9
WA7: Nort ... 1B 52
BLACKBROOK ... 2H 21
Blackbrook Av. WA2: Warr ... 5G 9
Blackbrook Cl. WA8: Wid ... 2E 27
Blackbrook Sq. WA2: Warr ... 1H 21
Blackburne Av. WA8: Hale B ... 2D 38
Blackburne Cl. WA2: P'gate ... 1B 22
Blackcap Wlk. WA3: Bchwd ... 6E 11
Black Cat Ind. Est. WA8: Wid ... 1H 39
Black Denton's Pl. WA8: Wid ... 4C 28
Blackheath La. WA7: Mnr P ... 3C 42
Blackhurst St. WA1: Warr ... 6D 20
Blackledge Cl. WA2: Fearn ... 6A 10
Blackley Cl. WA4: Latch ... 2F 33
Blackshaw Dr. WA5: W'brk ... 2F 19
Blair Dr. WA8: Wid ... 2D 26
Blandford Rd. WA5: Gt San ... 6F 19
Blantyre St. WA7: Run ... 4H 39
Blenheim Cl. WA2: P'gate ... 1G 21
Bloomsbury Way WA8: Wid ... 2F 27
Bluebell Ct. WA7: Beech ... 5F 51
Blue Bri. La. WA6: Hel ... 6E 55
Bluecoat St. WA2: Warr ... 4D 20
Blue Hatch WA6: Frod ... 3C 56
Blue Ridge Cl. WA5: Gt San ... 4C 18
Blundell Rd. WA8: Wid ... 5E 27
BLUNDELL'S HILL ... 1D 14
Blundell's La. L35: R'hill ... 2C 14
Blyth Cl. WA7: Murd ... 4B 52
Blythe Av. WA8: Wid ... 1B 28
Boat Stage WA13: Lymm ... 2C 36
Boat Wlk. WA4: Warr ... 4C 32
Bob's La. M44: Cad ... 5H 13
Bodmin Cl. WA7: Brook ... 3H 51
BOLD ... 2A 6
Bold Bus. Cen. WA9: Bold ... 2A 6
BOLD HEATH ... 4E 17
Bold Ind. Est. WA8: Wid ... 6C 16
Bold Ind. Pk. WA9: Bold ... 3A 6
Bold La. WA5: C Grn ... 2A 6
WA9: Bold ... 2A 6
Bold St. WA1: Warr ... 6C 20
WA7: Run ... 4B 40
(not continuous)
WA8: Wid ... 6A 28
Boleyn Ct. WA7: Mnr P ... 4A 42
Bollin Cl. WA3: Cul ... 5G 5
WA13: Lymm ... 1E 37
Bollin Dr. WA13: Lymm ... 1E 37
Bolton Av. WA4: Westy ... 1H 33
Bond Cl. WA5: Warr ... 1H 31
Booth's Cl. CH2: Elt ... 3E 59
Booths Hill Cl. WA13: Lymm ... 3B 36
Booth's Hill Rd.
WA13: Lymm ... 2A 36
Booth's La. WA13: Lymm ... 3H 35
Booth St. WA5: Warr ... 1A 32
Borrowdale Av. WA2: Warr ... 6E 9
Borrowdale Cl. WA6: Frod ... 3D 56
Borrowdale Rd. WA8: Wid ... 5E 27
Bostock St. WA5: Warr ... 5A 20
Boston Av. WA7: Run ... 1B 50
Boston Blvd. WA5: Gt San ... 4E 19
Boston Cl. WA3: Cul ... 3F 5
Boswell Av. WA4: Warr ... 3D 32
Boteler Av. WA5: Warr ... 4B 20
Bouchier Way WA4: Grap ... 5A 34
Boulting Av. WA5: Warr ... 1B 20
Boundary St. WA1: Warr ... 4G 21
Bournemouth Cl. WA7: Murd ... 3B 52
Boverton Cl. WA5: Call ... 2A 20
Bowden Cl. WA3: Cul ... 3F 5
Bowdon Cl. WA1: P'gate ... 3H 21
Bowen Cl. WA8: Wid ... 1F 27
Bower Cres. WA4: S'ton ... 5F 45
Bowers Bus. Pk. WA8: Wid ... 6B 28
Bowers Pk. Ind. Est.
WA8: Wid ... 6C 28
Bower St. WA8: Wid ... 4C 28
Bowland Av. WA9: Sut M ... 1B 16
Bowland Cl. WA3: Bchwd ... 4H 11
WA7: Beech ... 4E 51
Bowman Av. WA4: Westy ... 6A 22
Bowness Av. M44: Cad ... 5H 13
WA2: Warr ... 1E 21
Bowood Ct. WA2: Win ... 5C 8
Boxgrove Cl. WA8: Wid ... 2B 28
Box Wlk. M31: Part ... 6H 13
Boydell Av. WA4: Grap ... 3B 34
WA4: Westy ... 1H 33
Boyle Av. WA2: Warr ... 2G 21
Bracken Cl. WA3: Bchwd ... 4C 10
Brackendale CH2: Elt ... 2F 59
WA7: Run ... 1D 50
Brackens, The WA4: Dares ... 6E 43
Bracken Way WA6: Frod ... 5C 56
Brackenwood Dr. WA8: Wid ... 6C 26
Brackenwood Gro. L35: Whis ... 1B 14
Brackenwood M. WA4: Grap ... 4C 34
Brackley Av. M44: Cad ... 3H 13
Brackley Cl. WA7: Run ... 4H 39
Brackley St. WA4: S Hth ... 4E 33
WA7: Run ... 4H 39
Bradgate Cl. WA5: Warr ... 5B 20
BRADLEY ... 4E 57
Bradley Blvd. WA5: Gt San ... 5F 19
Bradley La. WA5: B'wood ... 1E 7
WA6: Frod ... 5D 56
Bradley Way WA8: Wid ... 4B 28
Bradshaw La. WA4: Grap ... 2B 34
WA13: Lymm ... 2H 37
Bradshaw St. WA8: Wid ... 3A 28
Braemar Cl. L35: Whis ... 1B 14
WA2: Fearn ... 6A 10
Braithwaite Cl. WA7: Beech ... 3D 50
Bramble Cl. WA5: Penk ... 2C 30
Bramble Way WA7: Beech ... 5E 51
Brambling Cl. WA7: Beech ... 4F 51
Bramhall St. WA5: Warr ... 6A 20
(not continuous)
Bramley M. WA4: S Hth ... 5E 33
Bramley Wlk. WA6: Hel ... 4C 60
Bramshill Cl. WA3: Bchwd ... 3G 11
Brandon WA8: Wid ... 3C 26
Brandwood Av. WA2: Warr ... 1D 20
Brandwood Ho. WA1: Warr ... 6E 21
Bransdale Cl. WA5: Gt San ... 4C 18
Brant Field Ct. WA2: Warr ... 1G 21
Brathay Cl. WA2: Warr ... 6E 9
Bray Cl. WA7: Beech ... 3D 50
Breck Rd. WA8: Wid ... 4B 28
Brecon Ct. WA5: Call ... 1A 20
Brendon Av. WA2: Warr ... 6C 8
Brentfield WA8: Wid ... 3F 27
Brentnall Cl. WA5: Gt San ... 6G 19
Brentwood Av. M44: Cad ... 3H 13
Brereton Cl. WA7: Cas ... 1G 51
(not continuous)
Bretland Dr. WA4: Grap ... 6A 34
Brian Av. WA2: Warr ... 3F 21
WA4: S Hth ... 4G 33
Briar Av. WA3: Rix ... 1F 25
Briarfield Av. WA8: Wid ... 4C 26
Briars Cl. L35: R'hill ... 2F 15
Briarswood Cl. L35: Whis ... 1B 14
Briarwood WA7: Nort ... 1A 52
Briarwood Av. WA1: Warr ... 4G 21
Brickhurst Way WA1: W'ston ... 3B 22
Brick St. WA1: Warr ... 6E 21
Bridge Av. WA4: Westy ... 1H 33
Bridge Av. E. WA4: Westy ... 6H 21
Bridge Cl. WA13: Lymm ... 2F 37
Bridge Ct. WA9: Clock F ... 1D 16
Bridge La. WA1: W'ston ... 5C 22
WA4: App ... 5G 33
WA6: Frod ... 2C 56
Bridgeman St. WA5: Warr ... 1H 31
Bridgend Cl. WA8: Wid ... 2F 27
Bridge Rd. WA1: W'ston ... 4C 22
WA9: Clock F ... 1D 16
Bridgeside Dr. WA6: Hel ... 1D 60
Bridge St. WA1: Warr ... 6D 20
WA7: Run ... 4B 40
Bridge Vw. Cl. WA8: Wid ... 3A 40
Bridge Wlk. *WA7: Pal F ... 2F 51*
(off Halton Lea Shop. Cen.)
Bridgewater Av. WA4: Westy ... 1H 33
Bri. Water Grange
WA7: Pres B ... 4D 52
Bridgewater M. WA4: S Hth ... 5E 33
Bridgewater Pl. WA3: Ris ... 4E 11
Bridgewater St. WA7: Run ... 4A 40
WA13: Lymm ... 2C 36
Bridgeway E. WA7: Wind H ... 5A 42
Bridgeway W. WA7: Wind H ... 5H 41
Bridlemere Ct. WA1: P'gate ... 3G 21
Briers Cl. WA2: Fearn ... 6H 9
Brighton St. WA5: Warr ... 5A 20
Brightwell Cl. WA5: Gt San ... 5C 18
Brimelow Cres. WA5: Penk ... 2C 30
Brindley, The ... 5A 40
Brindley Av. WA4: Westy ... 1H 33
Brindley Ct. WA4: S Hth ... 5F 33
Brindley Rd. WA7: Ast ... 4F 41
Brindley St. WA7: Run ... 4H 39

64 A-Z Warrington

Chatfield Dr. WA3: Bchwd 6E 11
Chatsworth Av. WA3: Cul 3F 5
Chatsworth Dr. WA8: Wid 2E 27
Chatteris Pk. WA7: Nort 5B 42
Chatterton Dr. WA7: Murd ...1C 52
Chaucer Pl. WA4: Westy 1H 33
Chaucer St. WA7: Run 6A 40
Cheddar Gro. WA5: B'wood ...2D 6
Chedworth Dr. WA8: Wid 1E 27
Chelford Cl. WA4: S Hth 5E 33
Chelsea Gdns. WA5: Gt San ...1G 31
Cheltenham Cl. WA5: Gt San ..3E 19
Cheltenham Cres. WA7: Run ..3B 50
Chepstow Cl. WA5: Call 6A 8
Cherry Blossom Rd.
  WA7: Beech 5F 51
Cherry Cnr. WA13: Lymm 1G 47
Cherry La. WA13: Lymm 6G 35
Cherrysutton WA8: Wid 2C 26
Cherry Tree Av. WA5: Penk ...1D 30
  WA7: Run 1C 50
  WA13: Lymm 3B 36
Cherry Tree Cl. CH2: Elt 1F 59
  L24: Hale 6A 38
Cherry Wlk. M31: Part 1H 25
  (not continuous)
Cherwell Cl. WA2: Warr 1F 21
Cheryl Dr. WA8: Wid 4D 28
Chesford Grange
  WA1: W'ston 4E 23
Cheshire Rd. M31: Part 1H 25
Cheshyre Dr. WA7: Halt 6F 41
Cheshyres La. WA1: Warr 6C 20
  WA7: West, West P 2G 49
  (not continuous)
Chessington Cl. WA4: App 1H 45
Chester Cl. M44: Cad 4H 13
  WA7: Cas 5F 41
Chester New Rd.
  WA4: H Walt 1A 44
Chester Rd. WA4: Dares 5G 43
  (Daresbury La., not continuous)
  WA4: Dares 4C 52
  (Red Brow La.)
  WA4: H Walt, Walt, Warr ..3C 32
  WA4: S Hth 4G 33
  WA6: Dun H 6A 60
  WA6: Frod, Hel 4C 60
  WA7: Sut W, Pres B 1F 57
Chester Row WA12: New W 1H 7
Chester St. WA2: Warr 5D 20
  WA8: Wid 4B 28
Chesterton Dr. WA2: Win 4C 8
Chestnut Av. M44: Cad 4H 13
  WA5: Gt San 5D 18
  WA8: Wid 3B 28
Chestnut Cl. WA8: Wid 4F 27
Chestnut Ho. WA4: App 6G 33
Chestnut La. WA6: Frod 1G 61
Chestnut Wlk. M31: Part 1H 25
Cheswood Rd. L35: Whis 1A 14
Chetham Ct. WA2: Win 6C 8
Chetwood Dr. WA8: Wid 6H 15
Cheviot Av. WA2: Warr 6C 8
Chichester Cl. WA4: Grap 6A 34
  WA7: Murd 3B 52
Chidlow Cl. WA8: Wid 2A 40
Chilington Av. WA8: Wid 5F 27
Chiltern Cres. WA2: Warr 6C 8
Chiltern Pl. WA2: Warr 6C 8
Chiltern Rd. WA2: Warr 6C 8
  WA3: Cul 3E 5
Chilwell Cl. WA8: Wid 1F 27
China La. WA4: Grap 3E 33
Chippindall Cl. WA5: Gt San ..6G 19
Chislet Cl. WA8: Wid 1G 27
Chiswick Cl. WA7: Murd 2B 52
Chiswick Gdns. WA4: App 1H 45
Cholmondeley Rd.
  WA7: Clftn 5D 50
Cholmondeley St. WA8: Wid ..3A 40
Chorley's La. WA8: Wid 2D 28
Chorley St. WA2: Warr 5E 21
  (Chester St.)
  WA2: Warr 5D 21
  (Norman St.)
Chorlton Cl. WA7: Wind H 6B 42
Christie St. WA8: Wid 4D 28
Christleton Ct. WA7: Mnr P ...3A 42
Christopher Cl. WA1: W'ston ..1H 21
Church Dr. WA2: P'gate 2A 22
Church End L24: Hale 6B 48

Church End M. L24: Hale 6B 48
Churchfield Rd. WA6: Frod ...3C 56
Churchfields WA3: Croft 2B 10
  WA6: Hel 1E 61
  WA8: Wid 6B 16
Church Grn. WA13: Warb 3F 25
Churchill Av. WA3: Cul 3H 5
Churchill Mans. WA7: Run ...4A 40
  (off Cooper St.)
Church La. WA3: Cul 4F 5
  WA4: Grap 4B 34
Church Mdw. Wlk.
  WA8: Hale B 2D 38
Church Rd. L24: Hale 6A 38
  WA6: Frod 4C 56
  WA13: Lymm 2B 36
Church St. WA1: Warr 6E 21
  WA6: Frod 3B 56
  WA7: Run 4A 40
  WA8: Wid 2A 40
Church St. Ind. Est.
  WA1: Warr 6E 21
Church Vw. WA6: K'ley 5G 57
  WA13: Lymm 1F 37
Church Wlk. WA2: Win 3C 8
Church Way WA6: Alv 4F 61
Churchwood Vw.
  WA13: Lymm 2D 36
Cinder La. WA4: Thel 3F 35
Cineworld Multiplex Cinema ..2F 51
CINNAMON BROW 6H 9
Cinnamon La. WA2: Fearn 6H 9
Cinnamon La. Nth.
  WA2: Fearn 5H 9
Cinnamon Pk. WA2: Fearn ...6B 10
Clamley Gdns. L24: Hale 5A 38
Clanfield Av. WA8: Wid 2E 27
Clapgate Cres. WA8: Hale B ..2D 38
Clap Gates Cres. WA5: Warr ..4A 20
Clap Gates Rd. WA5: Warr ...4A 20
Claremont Av. WA8: Wid 1C 28
Claremont Dr. WA8: Wid 1B 28
Claremont Rd. WA3: Cul 3D 4
  WA7: Run 5B 40
Clarence Av. WA5: Gt San 5B 18
  WA8: Wid 1A 28
Clarence Rd. WA4: Grap 3B 34
Clarence St. WA1: Warr 4G 21
  WA7: Run 4H 39
Clarence Ter. WA7: Run 4A 40
Clarendon Cl. WA7: Murd 2B 52
Clarendon Ct. WA2: Win 5B 8
Clares Farm Cl. WA1: W'ston .4F 23
Clarke Av. WA3: Cul 3F 5
  WA4: Latch 3F 33
  (not continuous)
Clarke Gdns. WA8: Wid 6B 28
Clarks Ter. WA7: West P 1F 49
Claude St. WA1: Warr 5E 21
Claverton Ct. WA7: Run 3B 50
Claydon Gdns. WA3: Rix 2D 24
Clay La. WA5: B'wood 3C 6
Clayton Cres. WA7: Run 6H 39
  WA8: Wid 4H 27
Clayton Rd. WA3: Ris 3F 11
Cleadon Way WA8: Wid 1G 27
Cleethorpes Rd. WA7: Murd ..2A 52
Cleeves Cl. WA1: Warr 6E 21
Clegge St. WA2: Warr 4D 20
Clelland St. WA4: Warr 2E 33
Cleveland Rd. WA2: Warr 6D 8
Cleveleys Av. WA8: Wid 3D 28
Cleveleys Rd. WA5: Gt San ...1F 31
Cliffe Rd. WA5: App 6E 33
Cliffe St. WA8: Wid 4C 28
Cliff La. WA4: Grap 1F 47
  (Grappenhall La.)
  WA4: Grap 3C 34
  (Knutsford Rd.)
  WA13: Lymm 1H 47
Clifford Rd. WA5: Penk 1E 31
Clifton Av. WA3: Cul 4D 4
Clifton Cres. WA6: Frod 2C 56
Clifton La. WA7: Clftn 5D 50
  (not continuous)
Clifton Rd. WA7: Run 2A 50
  WA7: Sut W 6E 51
Clifton St. WA2: Warr 1E 33
Cliftonville Rd. WA1: W'ston ..4C 22

Clincton Cl. WA8: Wid 5C 26
Clincton Vw. WA8: Wid 5C 26
Clive Av. WA2: Warr 2E 21
Clock Face Rd. WA8: Bold H ..1D 16
  WA9: Clock F 1D 16
Clock La. WA8: Wid 2F 29
Clough, The WA7: Halt 6F 41
Clough Av. WA2: Warr 1D 20
Clovelly Av. WA5: Gt San 4C 18
Clovelly Gro. WA7: Brook 4H 51
Clover Av. WA6: Frod 4D 56
Clover Ct. WA7: Brook 4H 51
Cloverfield WA7: Nort 2A 52
  WA13: Lymm 1D 36
Clydesdale Rd. WA4: App 5F 33
Cobal Ct. WA6: Frod 3B 56
COBBS 5F 33
Cobbs La. WA4: App 5F 33
Cobden St. WA4: Warr 5D 20
Cock Glade L35: Whis 2A 14
Cockhedge Grn. WA1: Warr ..5E 21
Cockhedge La. WA1: Warr ...6E 21
Cockhedge Shopping Pk.
  WA1: Warr 6D 20
Cockhedge Way WA1: Warr ..6D 20
Cockade La. L24: Hale 6B 48
Cockla La. Ends WA8: Hale B .3D 38
Coldstream Cl. WA2: Warr ...5G 9
Colebrooke Cl. WA3: Bchwd ..5G 11
Coleclough Pl. WA3: Cul 3F 5
Colemere Cl. WA1: P'gate ...2A 22
Coleridge Gro. WA8: Wid 5G 27
College Cl. WA7: Run 6F 21
  WA2: Fearn 5H 9
College Pl. WA3: P'gate 1B 22
Collier's Row WA7: West 2G 49
Collier St. WA7: Run 4H 39
COLLINS GREEN 1B 6
Collins Grn. La. WA5: C Grn ..1C 6
Collinson Ct. WA6: Frod 3B 56
Collin St. WA5: Warr 6A 20
Colne Rd. WA5: B'wood 3D 6
Colorado Cl. WA5: Gt San ...4G 19
Columbine Cl. WA8: Wid 1D 26
Colville Ct. WA2: Win 6C 8
Colwyn Cl. WA5: Call 1A 20
Common, The WA7: Halt 6G 41
Common La. WA3: Cul 3D 4
  WA4: Latch 3G 33
  WA4: Lwr S 4G 33
  WA6: Hap 4H 59
Commonside WA6: Alv 3F 61
Company's Cl. WA7: West 3H 49
Compass Cl. WA7: Murd 4B 52
Concord Pl. WA7: Run 1F 21
Conery Cl. WA6: Hel 1E 61
Coney Gro. WA7: Brook 4G 51
Conifer Gro. WA4: Moore 6E 31
Conifer Wlk. M31: Part 6H 13
Coniston Av. WA5: Penk 1B 30
Coniston Cl. WA7: Beech 3D 50
Coniston Dr. WA6: Frod 3C 56
Connaught Av. WA1: Warr ...4G 21
Conroy Way WA12: New W ...1G 7
Constables Cl. WA7: Cas 6G 41
Constance Way WA8: Wid ...1A 40
Conway Av. WA5: Warr 1B 20
Conway Cl. WA5: Gt San 5D 18
Conway Ct. WA7: Cas 5G 41
Coogee Av. WA5: Gt San 4C 18
Coombe Dr. WA7: Run 1H 49
Cooper Av. WA2: Warr 1D 20
Coopers Pl. WA4: Warr 4E 33
Cooper St. WA7: Run 4A 40
  WA8: Wid 4B 28
Copeland Gro. WA7: Beech ..4E 51
Copeland Rd. WA4: Warr 3D 32
Copperfield Cl. WA3: Bchwd ..4C 10
Copperwood WA7: Nort 6A 42
Copperwood Dr. L35: Whis ...1A 14
Coppice Cl. WA7: Cas 6H 41
Coppice Grn. CH2: Elt 1F 59
Coppins, The WA7: Murd 1E 21
Copse, The WA7: Pal F 3G 51
  (not continuous)
Corbet Av. WA2: Warr 3D 20
Corbet St. WA2: Warr 3D 20
Cormorant Cen., The
  WA7: Run 5G 39
Cormorant Rd. WA7: Run 5G 39

Cornerhouse La. WA8: Wid ...2F 27
Cornforth Way WA8: Wid 2H 27
Cornmill Cl. WA3: Croft 1A 10
Cornubia Rd. WA8: Wid 6C 28
Cornwall Av. WA7: Run 5A 40
Cornwall Cl. WA7: Cas 6F 41
Cornwall Rd. M44: Cad 4H 13
  WA8: Wid 2B 28
Cornwall St. WA1: Warr 4G 21
Coronation Av. WA3: G'bury ..6H 5
  WA4: Grap 3C 34
Coronation Dr. WA5: Penk ...1D 30
  WA6: Frod 2D 56
  WA8: Wid 5D 26
Coronation Ho. WA7: Run 1C 50
Coronation Rd. WA7: Pres B ..3D 52
  WA7: Run 6B 40
Coroner's La. WA8: Wid 6A 16
Coronet Way WA8: Wid 5D 26
Corwen Cl. WA5: Call 2A 20
Cossack Av. WA2: Warr 2D 20
Cote Lea Ct. WA7: Pal F 3F 51
Cotswold Pl. WA2: Warr 5D 8
Cotswold Rd. WA2: Warr 5D 8
Cotterdale Cl. WA5: Gt San ...4D 18
Cotterill WA7: Run 1D 50
Cotterill Dr. WA1: W'ston 4C 22
Cottham Dr. WA7: Fearn 6A 10
Cotton La. WA7: Run 1D 50
Coulton Rd. WA8: Wid 2E 29
Coverdale Av. L35: R'hill 1F 15
Coverdale Cl. WA5: Gt San ...4D 18
Cowan Way WA8: Wid 1H 27
Cowdell St. WA2: Warr 4D 20
Cow Hey La. WA7: Clftn 4A 50
Coylton Av. L35: R'hill 1F 15
Crab La. WA2: Fearn 6A 10
Crab Tree Cl. L24: Hale 5A 38
Crabtree Fold WA7: Nort 1A 52
Crabtree La. WA13: Lymm ...6E 37
  WA16: H Legh 6E 37
Cradley WA8: Wid 3E 27
Cranage Cl. WA7: Run 2D 50
Cranborne Av. WA4: Warr ...4C 32
Cranford Ct. WA1: W'ston ...3E 23
Cranleigh Cl. WA4: S Hth 6D 32
Cranshaw Av. WA9: Clock F ..1D 16
Cranshaw La. WA8: Wid 6B 16
Cranwell Av. WA3: Cul 3F 5
Craven Cl. WA2: Win 5B 8
Craven Rd. L35: R'hill 1E 15
Crawford Av. WA8: Wid 4D 26
Crawford Pl. WA7: Run 3B 50
Crawley Av. WA2: Warr 6C 8
Crescent, The WA13: Lymm ..3D 36
Crescent Av. WA6: Hel 2D 60
Cressbrook Rd. WA4: S Hth ..5E 33
Cresswell Cl. WA5: Call 6H 7
Cresta Dr. WA7: West 3H 49
Croasdale Dr. WA7: Beech ...4E 51
CROFT 2A 10
Croft, The WA6: Alv 5G 61
  WA7: Halt 6F 41
Croft Av. WA4: Grap 6A 34
CROFT HEATH 1A 10
Cft. Heath Gdns.
  WA3: Croft 1A 10
Croft Ho. WA3: Croft 2A 10
Crofton Cl. WA4: App T 2C 46
Crofton Gdns. WA3: Cul 4E 5
Crofton Rd. WA7: Run 6G 39
Croftside WA1: W'ston 4F 23
Croft St. WA8: Wid 1A 40
Croftwood Gro. L35: Whis ...1A 14
Cromdale Way WA5: Gt San ..5C 18
Crompton Dr. WA2: Win 3C 8
Crompton La. L35: R'hill 3D 14
Cromwell Av. WA2: Warr 6A 8
  WA5: Gt San, Old H, W'brk
  ....1G 19
Cromwell Av. Sth.
  WA5: Gt San 1G 31
Cromwell Cl. WA1: Warr 6C 20
  (off Arpley St.)
Cromwell St. WA8: Wid 1A 40
CRONTON 6E 15
Cronton Farm Ct. WA8: Wid ..1G 27
Cronton La. L35: R'hill 1D 14
  WA8: Wid 3D 14
  WA8: Wid 6G 15
Cronton Pk. Av. WA8: Cron ...5E 15
Cronton Pk. Cl. WA8: Cron ...5E 15

Cronton Rd.—Eccles Gro.

onton Rd. L35: Tar G 4A 14
WA8: Cron 6D 14
onulla Dr. WA5: Gt San 4B 18
oppers Rd. WA2: Fearn 6H 9
osby Av. WA5: Warr 3B 20
osfield St. WA1: Warr 6C 20
oss, The WA6: K'ley 5H 57
WA13: Lymm 2C 36
ossfield Av. WA3: Cul 5F 5
WA13: Lymm 2D 36
oss Gates WA8: Wid 2F 29
oss Hillocks La. WA8: Wid 3A 26
ossland M. WA13: Lymm 1H 35
ossland Ter. WA6: Hel 3D 60
oss La. WA3: Croft 2C 10
WA4: Grap 3A 34
WA6: Frod 3D 54
oss La. Sth. WA3: Ris 3E 11
rossley St. WA1: Warr 5E 21
ross St. WA2: Warr 4D 20
WA7: Run 4A 40
WA8: Wid 4B 28
(not continuous)
ossway WA8: Wid 4F 27
oston Cl. WA8: Wid 2E 27
rouchley Hall M.
WA13: Lymm 4D 36
rouchley La. WA13: Lymm 3C 36
rowe Av. WA2: Warr 1D 20
rowley La. WA16: H Legh 4G 47
rown Av. WA8: Wid 5D 26
rown Ga. WA7: Pal F 2F 51
rown Grn. WA13: Lymm 1F 37
rown St. WA1: Warr 6D 20
ROW WOOD 3D 28
ow Wood La. WA8: Wid 3D 28
ow Wood Pl. WA8: Wid 2D 28
ryers La. CH2: Thor M 6D 58
UERDLEY CROSS 3G 29
uerdley Grn. WA5: Cuerd 3G 29
uerdley Rd. WA5: Penk 2A 30
uerdon Dr. WA4: Thel 4D 34
ulbin Cl. WA3: Bchwd 3G 11
ULCHETH 5G 5
ulcheth Hall Dr. WA3: Cul 3F 5
ulford Cl. WA7: Wind H 6B 42
ullen Rd. WA7: West P 2F 49
umberland Av. M44: Cad 5G 13
umberland Rd. M31: Part 1H 25
umberland St. WA4: Warr 2E 33
umber La. L35: Whis 1B 14
unliffe Cl. WA7: Pal F 2G 51
unningham Cl.
WA5: Gt San 6D 18
unningham Dr. WA7: Run 1G 49
unningham Rd. WA8: Wid 5F 27
urlender Way L24: Hale 5A 38
urlew Gro. WA3: Bchwd 6E 11
urrans Rd. WA2: Warr 1D 20
urzon Dr. WA4: Grap 6A 34
urzon St. WA7: Run 6H 39
ygnet Ct. WA1: Warr 2C 32
ynthia Av. WA1: W'ston 4B 22
ynthia Rd. WA7: Run 5H 39
ypress Av. WA8: Wid 2B 28
ypress Cl. WA1: W'ston 4E 23
ypress Gro. WA7: Run 2C 50
yril Bell Cl. WA13: Lymm 2D 36
yril St. WA2: Warr 4D 20

D

Dacres Bri. La. L35: Tar G 5A 14
Daffodil Cl. WA8: Wid 1E 29
Dagnall Av. WA5: Warr 1B 20
Dairy Bank CH2: Elt 1F 59
Dairy Farm Cl. WA13: Lymm 2D 36
Daisy Bank Mill Cl. WA3: Cul 4E 5
Daisy Bank Rd. WA5: Penk 1D 30
WA13: Lymm 2A 36
Dakota Dr. WA5: Gt San 4G 19
Dalby Cl. WA3: Bchwd 4H 11
Dale, The WA5: Gt San, Penk 6D 18
Dale Cl. WA5: Warr 1A 32
WA8: Wid 5C 26
Dalecroft WA6: Hap 4A 60
Dale Gro. M44: Cad 3H 13
Dale La. WA4: App 5G 33
(not continuous)
Dale St. WA7: Run 6A 40
Dalewood Cl. WA2: Warr 5C 20
Dalewood Cres. CH2: Elt 2E 59
Dalewood Gdns. L35: Whis 1B 14
Dallam Ct. WA2: Warr 4C 20
Dallam La. WA2: Warr 4C 20
Dalton Av. WA3: Ris 3E 11
WA5: Warr 4B 20
Dalton Bank WA1: Warr 5E 21
Dalton Ct. WA7: Ast 4E 41
Dalton St. WA7: Run 5D 40
Dalwood Cl. WA7: Murd 2C 52
Dam Head La.
WA3: G'brk, Rix 5D 12
Dam La. WA1: W'ston 4D 22
WA3: Croft 2H 9
WA3: Rix 4C 12
Damson Wlk. M31: Part 6H 13
Danby Cl. WA5: Warr 4A 20
WA7: Beech 3D 50
Dane Bank Rd. WA13: Lymm 2C 36
Dane Bank Rd. E.
WA13: Lymm 1C 36
Danescroft WA8: Wid 2D 26
Daniel Adamson Av.
M31: Part 6H 13
Daniel Cl. WA3: Bchwd 5G 11
Dan's Rd. WA8: Wid 3E 29
DARESBURY 4F 43
Daresbury By-Pass
WA4: Dares 6F 43
Daresbury Ct. WA8: Wid 2D 28
Daresbury Expressway
WA4: Moore, Dares 3D 42
WA7: Run, Ast, Wind H, Nort
5A 40
Daresbury La.
WA4: Dares, Hatt 5G 43
Daresbury Pk. WA4: Dares 1E 53
Daresbury Science Pk.
WA4: Dares 4F 43
Dark La. WA6: K'ley 6G 57
Darley Av. WA2: Warr 6G 9
Darley Cl. WA8: Wid 2D 26
Darlington Ct. WA8: Wid 6A 28
Darnaway Cl. WA3: Bchwd 3H 11
Darwen Gdns. WA2: Warr 2G 21
Dashwood Cl. WA4: Grap 6A 34
Daten Av. WA3: Ris 3E 11
Davenham Av. WA1: P'gate 3G 21
Davenport Av. WA4: Westy 6H 21
Davenport Row WA7: Run 1D 50
David Lloyd Leisure 6H 19
David Rd. WA13: Lymm 2A 36
David's Av. WA5: Gt San 6F 19
Davies Av. WA4: Westy 1H 33
Davies Cl. WA8: Wid 3A 40
Davies Way WA13: Lymm 2C 36
Davy Av. WA3: Ris 4E 11
Davy Rd. WA7: Ast 4E 41
Dawlish Cl. WA3: Rix 6F 13
Dawson Ho. WA5: Gt San 5A 18
Deacon Rd. WA8: Wid 4B 28
Deacons Cl. WA3: Croft 1A 10
Deal Cl. WA5: Warr 4B 20
Dean Cl. WA8: Wid 5B 28
Dean Cres. WA2: Warr 1D 20
Dean Rd. M44: Cad 3H 13
Deansfield Way CH2: Elt 2E 59
DEANSGREEN 6F 37
Deans La. WA4: Thel 2F 35
Dean St. WA8: Wid 5B 28
Deansway WA8: Wid 5E 27
Deanwater Cl.
WA3: Bchwd 5D 10
Dean Way WA9: Sut M 1B 16
Deanwood Cl. L35: Whis 1B 14
Deepdale WA8: Wid 2E 27
Deepdale Cl. WA5: Gt San 4D 18
Deepdale Dr. L35: R'hill 1F 15
Deepwood Gro. L35: Whis 1A 14
Deer Pk. Ct. WA7: Pal F 3F 51
Deirdre Av. WA8: Wid 4A 28
De Lacy Row WA7: Cas 5G 41
Delafield Cl. WA2: Fearn 6H 9
Delamere Av. WA8: Wid 4E 27
WA9: Sut M 1A 16
Delamere St. WA5: Warr 6A 20
Delenty Dr. WA3: Ris 5D 10
Delery Dr. WA1: P'gate 3G 21
Dell Dr. WA2: Fearn 1A 22
Delphfield WA7: Nort 1B 52
Delphfields Rd. WA4: App 6E 33
Delph La. WA2: Hou G 2F 9
WA2: Win 5B 8
WA4: Dares 4E 43
Delta Cres. WA5: W'brk 1G 19
Delves Av. WA5: Warr 4B 20
Denbigh Cl. WA6: Hel 4C 60
Denbury Av. WA4: S Hth 3H 33
Denehurst Cl. WA5: Penk 1D 30
Denham Av. WA5: Gt San 6F 19
Denise Av. WA5: Penk 6C 18
Dennett Cl. WA1: W'ston 5E 23
Dennis Rd. WA8: Wid 6C 28
Densham Av. WA2: Warr 2D 20
Denton St. WA8: Wid 4C 28
Denver Dr. WA5: Gt San 4F 19
Denver Rd. WA4: Westy 2A 34
Derby Cl. M44: Cad 4G 13
Derby Dr. WA1: Warr 4G 21
Derby Rd. WA4: S Hth 5E 33
WA8: Wid 2A 28
Derby Row WA12: New W 1H 7
Derbyshire Rd. M31: Part 1H 25
Dereham Way WA7: Nort 4B 42
Derek Av. WA2: Warr 2F 21
Derwent Cl. WA3: Cul 5G 5
Derwent Rd. WA4: Warr 3D 32
WA8: Wid 4E 27
Desoto Rd. WA8: Wid 2F 39
Desoto Rd. E. WA8: Wid 1H 39
(not continuous)
Desoto Rd. W. WA8: Wid 1H 39
Devon Pl. WA8: Wid 2A 28
Devon Rd. M44: Cad 4H 13
Devonshire Pl. WA7: Run 4A 40
Devonshire Rd. WA1: P'gate 3H 21
Dewar Ct. WA7: Ast 4E 41
Dewar St. WA3: Ris 4E 11
Dewhurst Rd. WA3: Bchwd 6D 10
Dial St. WA1: Warr 6E 21
Dickenson St. WA2: Warr 4E 21
Dickson Cl. WA8: Wid 5B 28
Dickson St. WA8: Wid 5A 28
(not continuous)
Dig La. WA2: Fearn 5B 10
WA6: Frod 4A 56
Dingle, The WA13: Lymm 2C 36
Dingle Bank Cl.
WA13: Lymm 2C 36
Dingle La. WA4: App 1H 45
Dingleway WA4: App 5F 33
Dinnington Ct. WA8: Wid 2G 27
Ditchfield Pl. WA8: Wid 5D 26
Ditchfield Rd. WA5: Penk 2C 30
WA8: Wid 5C 26
DITTON 5E 27
Ditton Rd. WA8: Wid 1E 39
(not continuous)
Dixon St. WA1: Warr 6C 20
Dock Rd. WA8: Wid 2H 39
Dock St. WA8: Wid 2A 40
Dodgsley Dr. WA6: K'ley 6H 57
Doeford Cl. WA3: Cul 2D 4
DOE GREEN 2B 30
Dolmans La. WA1: Warr 6D 20
Domville L35: Whis 1A 14
Domville Cl. WA13: Lymm 2C 36
Dood's La. WA4: App 2A 46
Dorchester Pk. WA7: Nort 4B 42
Dorchester Rd. WA5: Gt San 6F 19
Dorchester Way WA5: B'wood 3D 6
Doric Av. WA6: Frod 4C 56
Dorney Cl. WA4: App 1G 45
Dornoch Ho. WA3: Ris 3D 10
Dorothea St. WA2: Warr 4E 21
Dorrington Cl. WA7: Murd 1B 52
Dorset Ct. WA7: Pal F 3G 51
Dorset Rd. M44: Cad 4H 13
Dorset Way WA1: W'ston 3B 22
Douglas Cl. WA8: Wid 2E 29
Dounrey Cl. WA2: Fearn 1A 22
Dove Cl. CH2: Elt 1G 59
WA3: Bchwd 5F 11
WA6: Hel 6E 55
Dovecote Grn. WA5: W'brk 1E 19
Dovedale Cl. WA2: Warr 6G 9
(not continuous)
Dovedale Ct. WA8: Wid 2D 26
Dover Cl. WA7: Murd 3C 52
Dover Rd. WA4: Westy 2A 34
Dover St. WA7: Run 4B 40
Doward St. WA8: Wid 3C 28
Downham Av. WA3: Cul 5F 5
Downside WA8: Wid 2D 26
Downs Rd. WA7: Run 6A 40
Dragon La. L35: Whis 1A 14
Dragon Yd. WA8: Wid 1B 28
Drake Av. M44: Cad 3H 13
Drake Cl. L35: Whis 1A 14
WA5: Old H 2H 19
Drayton Cl. WA7: Run 6H 39
Drive, The WA13: Lymm 4H 37
DriveTime (Golf Driving Range)
3C 32
Driveway L35: Whis 1B 14
Drovers La. WA6: Frod 6C 56
Drummond Ct. WA8: Wid 3D 28
Druridge Dr. WA5: Penk 1D 30
Dryden Pl. WA2: Warr 1E 21
Duckworth Gro. WA2: P'gate 2A 22
Dudley Av. WA7: Run 5D 40
Dudley Rd. M44: Cad 5H 13
Dudley St. WA2: Warr 4D 20
Dudlow Grn. Rd. WA4: App 2F 45
DUDLOW'S GREEN 1F 45
Duke Av. WA3: G'bury 6H 5
Duke Cl. WA7: Run 4H 39
Dukes Wharf WA7: Pres B 3C 52
Dunbeath Av. L35: R'hill 2F 15
Dunbeath Cl. L35: R'hill 2F 15
Duncan Av. WA7: Run 6C 40
Duncansby Cres.
WA5: Gt San 5C 18
Duncan St. WA2: Warr 4E 21
Dundalk La. WA8: Wid 5F 27
Dundalk Rd. WA8: Wid 5F 27
Dundee Cl. WA2: Fearn 5G 9
Dundonald Av. WA4: S Hth 4E 33
DUNHAM-ON-THE-HILL 6B 60
Dunham Rd. WA13: Warb 4H 25
Dunley Cl. WA3: Bchwd 3G 11
Dunlin Cl. WA2: Warr 6G 9
WA7: Beech 4F 51
Dunlop St. WA4: Warr 2D 32
Dunmail Gro. WA7: Beech 5E 51
Dunmow Rd. WA4: Thel 2C 34
Dunnock Cl. WA2: Warr 6G 9
Dunnock Gro. WA3: Bchwd 5E 11
Dunscar Cl. WA3: Bchwd 4D 10
Dunsford WA8: Wid 2D 26
Durham Cl. WA1: W'ston 4E 23
Durham Gro. M44: Cad 3G 13
Durham Rd. WA8: Wid 2B 28
Durlston Cl. WA8: Wid 3E 27
Dursley L35: Whis 1B 14
DUTTON 6E 53
Duxford Ct. WA2: P'gate 2G 21
Dyers Cl. WA13: Lymm 1E 37
Dyers La. WA13: Lymm 1E 37
Dykin Cl. WA8: Wid 2E 29
Dykin Rd. WA8: Wid 2D 28

E

Eagle Brow WA13: Lymm 2B 36
Eagle Mt. WA4: Warr 3E 33
Eagle Pk. Dr. WA2: Warr 2C 20
Eagles Way WA7: Pal F 3E 51
Ealing Cl. WA7: Nort 6B 42
Ealing Rd. WA5: Gt San 6E 19
Eanleywood La. WA7: Nort 1H 51
Earle Rd. WA8: Wid 6C 28
Earl St. WA2: Warr 4D 20
Earls Way WA7: Pal F 2E 51
Earlwood Gdns. L35: Whis 1A 14
Easby Cl. WA7: Run 5C 40
Easenhall Cl. WA8: Wid 1B 28
East Av. WA2: Warr 3E 21
WA4: S Hth 4F 33
WA5: Gt San 1E 31
Eastbury Cl. WA8: Wid 6C 16
Eastdale Rd. WA1: P'ton 4A 22
Easter Ct. WA5: W'brk 1F 19
Eastford Rd. WA4: Warr 4B 32
East Front L35: Whis 2A 14
Eastgate Way WA7: Mnr P 3B 42
E. Lancashire Rd.
WA12: New W 1A 4
East La. WA7: Pal F 2F 51
East St. WA8: Wid 4D 28
East Vw. WA4: Grap 3B 34
Eastway WA7: Pal F 2F 51
WA8: Wid 4F 27
Eastwood WA7: Wind H 6A 42
Eastwood Rd. WA5: B'wood 2D 6
Eaton St. WA7: Run 5A 40
Eaves Brow Rd. WA3: Croft 2B 10
Ebenezer Pl. WA1: Warr 6C 20
Eccles Gro. WA9: Clock F 1E 17

A-Z Warrington 67

Eccleston Cl.—Gala Bingo

Eccleston Cl. WA3: Bchwd 4C 10
Eccleston Dr. WA7: Run 6C 40
Eddarbridge Est. WA8: Wid 2H 39
Eddisbury Sq. WA6: Frod 3B 56
Eddisford Dr. WA3: Cul 2D 4
Edelsten St. WA5: Warr 6B 20
Eden Av. WA3: Cul 3H 5
Edenbridge Gdns. WA4: App ...4G 45
Eden Cl. L35: R'hill 1D 14
Edendale WA8: Wid 3D 26
Edgars Dr. WA2: Fearn 2A 22
Edgeworth St. WA2: Warr 5C 20
Edinburgh Rd. WA8: Wid 5C 26
Edison Rd. WA7: Ast 4D 40
Edith St. WA7: Run 4H 39
Edward Gdns. WA1: W'ston 5F 23
Edward Rd. WA5: Gt San 5B 18
Edward St. WA8: Wid 4D 28
Edwards Way WA8: Wid 5E 27
Edwin St. WA8: Wid 4C 28
Egdon Cl. WA8: Wid 3E 29
Egerton Av. WA1: Warr 4G 21
(not continuous)
WA13: Warb 3G 25
Egerton M. WA4: S Hth 4E 33
Egerton Rd. WA13: Lymm 3A 36
Egerton St. WA1: Warr 6F 21
WA4: S Hth 4E 33
WA7: Run 4H 39
Eglington Av. L35: Whis 1A 14
Egypt St. WA1: Warr 6D 20
WA8: Wid 6H 27
Eisenhower Cl. WA5: Gt San 5F 19
Elaine Cl. WA8: Wid 3C 28
Elaine Price Ct. WA7: Run 6H 39
Elaine St. WA1: Warr 4F 21
Eldon St. WA1: Warr 6E 21
Eleanor St. WA8: Wid 6A 28
Elgin Av. WA4: Warr 3C 32
Elgin Ct. L35: R'hill 1F 15
Elizabeth Ct. WA8: Wid 6B 28
Elizabeth Dr. WA1: P'gate 3A 22
Elizabeth Ter. WA8: Wid 4F 27
Elkan Cl. WA8: Wid 3E 29
Elkan Rd. WA8: Wid 3D 28
Ellen St. WA5: Warr 4B 20
Ellerby Cl. WA7: Murd 2C 52
Ellerton Cl. WA8: Wid 2E 27
Ellesmere Rd. WA3: Cul 3E 5
WA4: S Hth, Walt 4D 32
Ellesmere St. WA1: Warr 6E 21
(not continuous)
WA7: Run 5B 40
Ellesworth Cl. WA5: Old H 3G 19
Elliot St. WA8: Wid 5B 28
Elliott Av. WA1: Warr 4G 21
Ellis La. WA6: Frod 2D 56
Ellison St. WA1: Warr 6E 21
WA4: S Hth 4F 33
Ellis St. WA8: Wid 6A 28
Ellon Av. L35: R'hill 1F 15
Ellwood Cl. L24: Hale 5A 38
Elm Av. WA8: Wid 3B 28
Elm Gro. WA1: P'ton 4H 21
WA8: Wid 4B 28
Elmore Cl. WA7: Wind H 6B 42
Elm Ri. WA6: Frod 4C 56
Elm Rd. WA2: Win 5C 8
WA3: Rix 1E 25
WA5: Penk 1D 30
WA7: Run 1C 50
Elms, The WA7: Run 6H 39
Elmsett Cl. WA5: Gt San 6C 18
Elmswood Av. L35: R'hill 1F 15
Elm Tree Av. WA13: Lymm 3B 36
Elmtree Av. WA1: P'gate 3H 21
Elm Tree Rd. WA13: Lymm 3B 36
Elmwood WA7: Nort 1A 52
Elmwood Av. WA1: Warr 4G 21
Elstree Ct. WA8: Wid 1D 28
Eltham Cl. WA8: Wid 2E 29
Eltham Wlk. WA8: Wid 2E 29
ELTON 2F 59
Elton Cl. WA3: Bchwd 5C 10
ELTON GREEN 3E 59
Elton La. WA6: Hel 1H 59
Elton Lordship La.
WA6: Frod 5C 54
Elvington Cl. WA7: Sut W 6F 51
Elworth Av. WA8: Wid 6A 16
Ely Pk. WA7: Nort 5C 42
Embleton Gro. WA7: Beech 4E 51
Emily St. WA8: Wid 6A 28
Enfield Pk. Rd. WA2: Fearn 5H 9
Ennerdale Av. WA2: Warr 6D 8
Ennerdale Dr. WA6: Frod 3C 56
Ennis Cl. L24: Hale 5B 48
Enticott Rd. M44: Cad 4G 13
Enville St. WA4: Warr 1E 33
Epping Av. WA9: Sut M 1B 16
Epping Cl. L35: R'hill 1F 15
Epping Dr. WA1: W'ston 3D 22
Epsom Gdns. WA4: App 6G 33
Epworth Cl. WA5: B'wood 2D 6
Eric Av. WA1: P'gate 3G 21
Eric St. WA8: Wid 3C 28
Erindale Cres. WA6: Frod 5A 56
Erwood St. WA2: Warr 5D 20
Eskdale Av. WA2: Warr 6E 9
Eskdale Cl. WA7: Beech 4D 50
Essex Gdns. M44: Cad 5G 13
Euclid Av. WA4: Grap 3B 34
Europa Blvd. WA5: W'brk 1G 19
Eustace St. WA2: Warr 5C 20
Evans Pl. WA4: Warr 2F 33
Evelyn St. WA5: Warr 1H 31
Evenwood Cl. WA7: Mnr P 3C 42
Everite Rd. WA8: Wid 6D 26
Everite Rd. Ind. Est.
WA8: Wid 6D 26
Eversley WA8: Wid 3D 26
Eversley Cl. WA4: App 2H 45
WA6: Frod 5C 56
Evesham Cl. WA4: S Hth 5E 33
Exeley L35: Whis 1A 14
Exmouth Cres. WA7: Murd 3C 52
Exmouth Way WA5: B'wood 3D 6
Express Ind. Est. WA8: Wid 6C 26
Exwood Gro. L35: Whis 1B 14

F

Factory La. WA5: Warr 6B 20
WA8: Wid 2B 28
Fairbourne Cl. WA5: Call 6A 8
Fairbrother Cres. WA2: Warr ...1F 21
Fairburn Cl. WA8: Wid 2E 29
Fairclough Av. WA1: Warr 1E 33
Fairclough St. WA5: B'wood 3C 6
Fairfax Dr. WA7: Run 5D 40
Fairfield Gdns. WA4: S Hth 3G 33
Fairfield Rd. M44: Cad 4G 13
WA4: S Hth 4E 33
WA8: Wid 4B 28
WA13: Lymm 2D 36
Fairfield St. WA1: Warr 5E 21
Fairford Cl. WA5: Gt San 5F 19
Fairhaven Cl. WA5: Gt San 1F 31
Fairhaven Rd. WA8: Wid 3C 28
Fair Havens Ct. WA8: Wid 6B 28
Fairlie Dr. L35: R'hill 1F 15
Fairoak Ct. WA7: Pres B 6D 52
Fairoak La. WA7: Pres B 6D 52
Fairways WA4: App 2F 45
WA6: Frod 4D 56
Falcondale Rd. WA2: Win 3D 8
Falconers Grn. WA5: W'brk 1F 19
Falcons Way WA7: Pal F 3E 51
Falkirk Av. WA8: Wid 2G 27
Fallowfield WA7: Run 6D 40
Fallowfield Gro. WA2: P'gate ...2B 22
Falmouth Dr. WA5: Penk 2C 30
Falmouth Pl. WA7: Murd 3C 52
Falstone Cl. WA3: Bchwd 3H 11
Falstone Dr. WA7: Murd 2C 52
Fanner's La. WA16: H Legh 2H 47
(not continuous)
Faraday Rd. WA7: Ast 4D 40
Faraday St. WA3: Ris 3E 11
Faringdon Rd. WA2: Win 3D 8
Farm Ct. CH2: Elt 2F 59
Farmdale Dr. CH2: Elt 2E 59
Farmers La. WA5: B'wood 3E 7
Farm La. WA4: App 5G 33
Farmleigh Gdns.
WA5: Gt San 5G 19
Farmside Cl. WA5: Warr 4A 20
Farndale WA8: Wid 6A 16
Farndale Cl. WA5: Gt San 4D 18
Farnham Cl. WA4: App 6G 33
Farnhill Cl. WA7: Nort 1B 52
Farnley Cl. WA7: Wind H 6B 42
Farnworth Cl. WA8: Wid 1B 28
Farnworth Rd. WA5: Penk 1B 30
WA8: Wid 1E 29
Farnworth St. WA8: Wid 1B 28
Farrant St. WA8: Wid 5B 28
Farrell Rd. WA4: S Hth 5E 33
Farrell St. WA1: Warr 6E 21
Farthings, The WA13: Lymm ...1B 36
Fawley Rd. L35: R'hill 2G 15
FEARNHEAD 1A 22
Fearnhead Cross
WA2: P'gate 1H 21
Fearnhead La. WA2: Fearn 1A 22
Feeny St. WA9: Sut M 1B 16
Fenham Dr. WA5: Penk 1C 30
Fennel St. WA1: Warr 6E 21
Fenton Cl. WA8: Wid 2D 26
Fenwick La. WA7: Run 3D 50
Ferguson Dr. WA2: Warr 2F 21
Fernbank Cl. WA3: Ris 5E 11
Fern Cl. WA3: Bchwd 5D 10
Ferndale Av. CH2: Elt 2E 59
Ferndale Cl. WA1: W'ston 4C 22
WA8: Bold H 4E 17
Fernhurst WA7: Run 6D 40
Fernwood WA7: Nort 1H 51
Ferry La. WA4: Thel 1E 35
Ferryview Wlk. WA7: Cas 5F 41
Festival Av. WA2: Warr 1E 21
Festival Cres. WA2: Warr 1F 21
Festival Way WA7: Run 1C 50
FIDDLER'S FERRY 4B 30
Fiddlers Ferry Rd. WA8: Wid ...5C 28
Fiddler's Ferry Sailing Club ...4C 30
Fieldfare Cl. WA3: Bchwd 5F 11
Fieldgate WA8: Wid 6D 26
Fieldhouse Row WA7: Run 2D 50
Field La. WA4: App 1E 45
Fieldsway WA7: West 3A 50
Fieldview Dr. WA2: Warr 2E 21
Fieldway WA6: Frod 4C 56
WA8: Wid 3D 28
Fife Rd. WA1: Warr 4G 21
Fifth Av. WA7: Pal F 2F 51
Fildes Cl. WA5: Gt San 6G 19
Fillmore Gro. WA8: Wid 2H 27
Finch Cl. WA9: Clock F 1D 16
Finger Ho. La. WA8: Bold H 2D 16
Finlan Rd. WA8: Wid 6A 28
Finlay Av. WA5: Penk 2C 30
Finningley Ct. WA2: P'gate 2G 21
Finsbury Cl. WA5: Gt San 1G 31
Finsbury Pk. WA8: Wid 6C 16
Firbank CH2: Elt 2G 59
Firbank Cl. WA7: Wind H 6B 42
Firecrest Ct. WA1: Warr 2C 32
Fir Gro. WA1: P'ton 4H 21
Firman Cl. WA5: W'brk 2F 19
Firs La. WA4: App 2D 44
(not continuous)
Fir St. M44: Cad 3F 13
WA8: Wid 3C 28
Firtree Av. WA1: P'gate 3A 22
Fir Tree Cl. WA4: S'ton 6F 45
Fir Tree La. WA5: B'wood 2E 7
Fisher Av. L35: Whis 1A 14
WA2: Warr 2D 20
Fisherfield Dr. WA3: Bchwd 4G 11
Fisher Pl. L35: Whis 1A 14
Fisher St. WA7: Run 4B 40
Fitness First
Runcorn 2E 51
Fitzherbert St. WA2: Warr 4D 20
Fitzwalter Rd. WA1: W'ston 4D 22
Fitzwilliam Wlk. WA7: Cas 5G 41
FIVECROSSES 6D 56
Flander Cl. WA8: Wid 3E 27
Flavian Ct. WA7: Cas 6E 41
Flaxley Cl. WA3: Bchwd 4G 11
Fleetwood Cl. WA5: Gt San 1F 31
Fleetwood Wlk. WA7: Murd 2A 52
Fleming Dr. WA2: Win 3C 8
Fleming Ind. Est. *WA1: Warr ...6E 21*
(off Fennel St.)
Flers Av. WA4: Warr 2E 33
Fletchers La. WA13: Lymm 1D 36
Fletcher St. WA4: Warr 2D 32
Flint Gro. M44: Cad 3G 13
Florence St. WA4: Warr 2F 33
Florida Cl. WA5: Gt San 4G 19
Fluin La. WA6: Frod 2C 56
Folkestone Way WA7: Murd 2A 52
Folly La. WA5: Warr 4B 20
WA7: Run 6F 39
Forbes Cl. WA3: Bchwd 5E 11
Fordington Rd. WA5: Gt San 6F 19
Ford St. WA1: Warr 5F 2
Fordton Leisure Cen. 6C
Foreland Cl. WA5: Gt San 4A 1
Forest Gdns. M31: Part 6H 1
Forest Rd. WA9: Sut M 1A 1
Forest Wlk. *WA7: Pal F 2F 5*
(off Halton Lea Shop. Cer
Forge Cl. WA8: Cron 6E 1
Forge Rd. WA5: Gt San 6D 1
Forge Shop. Cen., The
WA4: S Hth 4E 3
Formby Cl. WA5: Penk 1D 3
Forrest Way WA5: Warr 2H 3
Forshaw's La. WA5: C Grn 1C
Forshaw St. WA2: Warr 4E 2
Forster St. WA2: Warr 4D 2
Foster St. WA8: Wid 4B 2
Fothergill St. WA1: Warr 4F 2
Foundry La. WA8: Hale B 2D 3
Foundry St. WA2: Warr 5D 2
Fountain La. WA6: Frod 3A 5
Fountains Cl. WA7: Brook 4A 5
Fourth Av. WA7: Pal F 2F 5
FOWLEY COMMON 3H
Fowley Comn. La. WA3: Cul 2H
Fox Bank Cl. WA8: Wid 1H 2
Foxcote WA8: Wid 3D 2
Fox Covert WA7: Nort 1A 5
Foxdale Ct. WA4: App 6F 3
Foxfield Cl. WA2: Warr 6G
Fox Gdns. WA13: Lymm 1A 3
Foxglove Ct. WA6: Frod 3C 5
Foxglove Dell WA6: Alv 3F 6
Foxhill Gro. WA6: Hel 1F 6
Foxhills Cl. WA4: App 4F 4
Foxley Cl. WA13: Lymm 3E 3
Foxley Hall M. WA13: Lymm ...4E 3
Foxley Heath WA8: Wid 5G 2
Fox's Bank La. L35: Whis 5B 1
Foxshaw Cl. L35: Whis 2A 1
Fox St. WA5: Warr 6A 2
WA7: Run 5A 4
Francis Cl. WA8: Wid 5E 2
Francis Rd. WA4: S Hth 4D 3
WA6: Frod 2C 5
Francis St. M44: Cad 4H 1
Franklin Cl. WA5: Old H 3G 1
Frank St. WA8: Wid 4C 2
Fraser Rd. WA5: Gt San 5B 1
Freckleton Cl. WA5: Gt San 1F 31
Frederick St. WA4: Latch 2F 3
WA8: Wid 4B 2
Frederick Ter. WA8: Hale B 3C 3
Fredric Pl. WA7: Run 4B 4
French St. WA8: Wid 4D 2
Freshfields Dr. WA2: P'gate 2B 22
Fresh Mdw. La. WA6: Hel 3D 60
Freshwater Cl. WA5: Gt San 4B 18
Friars Av. WA5: Gt San 6C 18
Friars Ga. WA1: Warr 1D 32
Friars La. WA1: Warr 1D 32
Friends La. WA5: Gt San 5B 18
Frobisher Ct. WA5: Old H 3H 19
Froda Av. WA6: Frod 4B 56
FRODSHAM 3B 56
Frodsham Bus. Cen.
WA6: Frod 2C 56
Frodsham Leisure Cen. 3B 56
Frodsham Pk. Homes
WA6: Frod 3A 56
Frodsham Rd. WA6: Alv 4F 61
Frodsham Station (Rail) 3B 56
Froghall La. WA1: Warr 6B 20
WA2: Warr 5C 20
WA13: H Legh, Lymm 5H 37
WA16: H Legh 5H 37
Fryer St. WA7: Run 4A 40
Fulbeck WA8: Wid 3E 27
Furness Ct. WA7: Nort 3D 42

G

Gables Cl. WA2: Fearn 6H 9
Gainford Cl. WA8: Wid 2E 27
Gainsborough Ct. WA8: Wid 4D 26
Gainsborough Rd.
WA4: Warr 3C 32
Gairloch Cl. WA2: Fearn 5H 9
Gaisgill Ct. WA8: Wid 4E 27
Gala Bingo
Warrington 6D 20
Widnes 5B 28

68 A-Z Warrington

H

Hamnett Ct.—Howley Quay

Hamnett Ct. WA3: Bchwd 6E **11**
Hampshire Rd. M31: Part 1H **25**
Hampson Av. WA3: Cul 4F **5**
Hampton Cl. WA8: Wid 2E **29**
Hampton Ct. WA7: Mnr P 3A **42**
Hampton Court Way
WA8: Wid 1D **28**
Hampton Dr. WA5: Gt San 1G **31**
WA8: Cron 6E **15**
Hampton Rd. M44: Cad 5H **13**
Hamsterley Cl. WA3: Bchwd . . .3H **11**
Hancock Ct. WA4: Warr 1E **33**
Handforth Cl. WA4: Thel 1D **34**
Handforth La. WA7: Run 3D **50**
Handley St. WA7: Run 4H **39**
Hankey St. WA7: Run 5H **39**
Hanley Cl. WA8: Wid 4E **27**
Hanley Rd. WA8: Wid 4E **27**
Hanover Ct. WA7: Brook 3H **51**
Hanover St. WA1: Warr 1C **32**
HAPSFORD **4A 60**
Hapsford Cl. WA3: Bchwd 5C **10**
Hapsford La. WA6: Hel 1G **59**
(Ash Rd.)
WA6: Hel 4A **60**
(Moor La.)
Harbord St. WA1: Warr 1E **33**
Harbour Cl. WA7: Murd 3B **52**
Harcourt Cl. WA3: Bchwd 6E **11**
Harding Av. WA2: Warr 2G **21**
Hardwick Grange
WA1: W'ston 2D **22**
Hardwick Rd. WA7: Ast 4D **40**
Hardy Rd. WA13: Lymm 3A **36**
Hardy St. WA2: Warr 5D **20**
(not continuous)
Harebell Cl. WA8: Wid 1G **27**
Hare's La. WA6: Frod 3G **55**
Harford Cl. WA5: Penk 1D **30**
Hargreaves Ct. WA8: Wid 4D **28**
Hargreaves Ho. *WA8: Wid 4D 28*
(off Hargreaves Ct.)
Harlech Cl. WA5: Call 1A **20**
Harlech Gro. WA7: Cas 6F **41**
Harlow Cl. WA4: Thel 2C **34**
Harlyn Gdns. WA5: Penk 2B **30**
Harpers Rd. WA2: P'gate 2A **22**
Harrier Rd. WA2: P'gate 1H **21**
Harriett St. M44: Cad 4H **13**
Harrison Cl. WA1: Warr 5E **21**
Harrison Sq. WA5: Warr 2B **20**
Harrison St. WA8: Hale B 1D **38**
Harris St. WA8: Wid 4C **28**
Harrogate Cl. WA5: Gt San 2E **19**
Harrop Rd. WA7: Run 6B **40**
Harrow Cl. WA4: App 1G **45**
Harrow Dr. WA7: Run 5E **41**
Hartland Cl. WA8: Wid 6A **16**
Hartley Cl. WA13: Lymm 2D **36**
Harton Cl. WA8: Wid 2G **27**
Hartswood Cl. WA4: App 4G **45**
Harvard Cl. WA7: Wind H 5B **42**
Harvard Ct. WA2: Win 6C **8**
Harvey Ct. WA2: Warr 6D **8**
Harwood Gdns. WA4: Grap 3A **34**
Haryngton Av. WA5: Warr 4B **20**
Haslemere L35: Whis 1B **14**
Haslemere Dr. WA5: Penk 1B **30**
Hastings Av. WA2: Warr 5D **8**
Hatchery Cl. WA4: App T 3B **46**
Hatchings, The WA13: Lymm . . .3D **36**
Hatchmere Cl. WA5: Warr 5A **20**
Hatfield Gdns. WA4: App 3G **45**
Hatley La. WA6: Frod 4G **55**
Hatters Row *WA1: Warr 6D 20*
(off Horsemarket St.)
HATTON **6C 44**
Hatton La. WA4: Hatt, S'ton 6C **44**
Havergal St. WA7: Run 6H **39**
Havisham Cl. WA3: Bchwd 4D **10**
Haweswater Cl. WA7: Beech 4G **51**
Hawks Ct. WA7: Pal F 3E **51**
Hawkshaw Cl. WA3: Bchwd 5C **10**
Hawkshead Cl. WA7: Beech 5G **51**
Hawkshead Rd.
WA5: B'wood 3C **6**
Hawkstone Gro. WA6: Hel 1E **61**
Hawley's Cl. WA5: Warr 2B **20**
Hawleys La. WA2: Warr 2B **20**
WA5: Warr 2B **20**
Hawthorn Av. WA7: Run 6A **40**
WA8: Wid 3B **28**
Hawthorn Dr. M44: Cad 4H **13**
Hawthorne Av. WA1: W'ston 4B **22**
WA5: Gt San 5D **18**
Hawthorne Bus. Pk.
WA5: Warr 3C **20**
Hawthorne Gro. WA1: P'ton 4H **21**
Hawthorne Rd. WA4: S Hth 5E **33**
WA6: Frod 2B **56**
WA13: Lymm 2B **36**
Hawthorne St. WA5: Warr 3C **20**
Hawthorn Gro. WA4: S Hth 4F **33**
WA4: Warr 2F **33**
Hawthorn Wlk. M31: Part 6H **13**
Haydock St. WA2: Warr 5D **20**
Hayes Cres. WA6: Frod 2C **56**
Hayes La. WA4: App 5G **33**
Haye's Rd. M44: Cad 4H **13**
Hayfield Rd. WA1: W'ston 4C **22**
Hayscastle Cl. WA5: Call 2A **20**
Haywood Cres. WA7: Wind H . . .5B **42**
Hazel Av. WA7: Run 1G **49**
Hazelborough Cl.
WA3: Bchwd 4H **11**
Hazel Dr. WA13: Lymm 3D **36**
Hazel Gro. WA1: P'ton 3A **22**
Hazel St. WA1: Warr 4F **21**
Hazel Wlk. M31: Part 6H **13**
Hazelwood Cl. WA8: Wid 5C **26**
Hazelwood M. WA4: Grap 4C **34**
Hazlehurst Rd. WA6: Frod 6C **56**
Heath, The WA7: West 2A **50**
Heath Dr. WA7: West 2A **50**
Heather Av. M44: Cad 3H **13**
Heather Cl. WA3: Bchwd 4D **10**
WA7: Beech 4E **51**
Heather Wlk. M31: Part 6H **13**
Heathfield Pk. WA4: Grap 3A **34**
WA8: Wid 2F **27**
Heath La. WA3: Croft 5A **4**
Heath Pk. Gro. WA7: Run 1H **49**
Heath Rd. WA5: Penk 6D **18**
WA7: Run, West 2H **49**
WA8: Wid 3F **27**
Heath Rd. Cres. WA7: Run 1B **50**
Heath Rd. Sth. WA7: West 3H **49**
Heath St. WA4: S Hth 5E **33**
Heathview Cl. WA8: Hale B 2C **38**
Heathview Rd. WA8: Hale B 2C **38**
Heathwood Gro. WA1: P'ton 4B **22**
HEATLEY **5G 25**
Heatley Cl. WA13: Lymm 1F **37**
Heaton Ct. WA3: Ris 3F **11**
Hebden Av. WA3: Cul 2H **5**
Hedge Hey WA7: Cas 6G **41**
Heights, The WA6: Hel 1E **61**
Helmsdale La. WA5: Gt San 5G **19**
Helmsley Cl. WA5: Warr 4A **20**
HELSBY **1E 61**
HELSBY MARSH **6D 54**
Helsby Pk. Homes
WA6: Frod 6G **55**
Helsby Rd. WA6: Alv 4E **61**
Helsby Sports & Social Club . . .**4C 60**
Helsby Station (Rail) **1D 60**
Helsby St. WA1: Warr 5F **21**
Helston Cl. WA5: Penk 6C **18**
WA7: Brook 4H **51**
Hemlegh Va. WA6: Hel 3D **60**
Henbury Gdns. WA4: App 4G **45**
Henbury Pl. WA7: Run 3B **50**
Henderson Cl. WA5: Gt San 5B **18**
Henderson Rd. WA8: Wid 5H **27**
Henley Cl. WA4: App 1G **45**
Henley Ct. WA7: Run 5D **40**
Henry St. WA1: Warr 6C **20**
WA8: Wid 4C **28**
WA13: Lymm 2C **36**
Henshall Av. WA4: Westy 1H **33**
Hepherd St. WA5: Warr 1H **31**
Heralds Cl. WA8: Wid 5D **26**
Heralds Grn. WA5: W'brk 1E **19**
Herbert St. WA5: B'wood 3C **6**
Hereford Cl. WA1: W'ston 4D **22**
Heritage Cen. **6B 32**
HERMITAGE GREEN **1D 8**
Hermitage Grn. La. WA2: Win . . .1B **8**
Heron Cl. WA7: Nort 1B **52**
Herons Way WA7: Nort 3D **42**
Hertford Cl. WA1: W'ston 4E **23**
Hertford Gro. M44: Cad 3G **13**
Hesketh Cl. WA5: Penk 1D **30**
Hesketh Rd. L24: Hale 5A **38**
Hesketh St. WA5: Warr 1H **31**
Hesketh St. Nth. WA5: Warr 1H **31**
Hesnall Cl. WA3: G'bury 5H **5**
Heswall Av. WA3: Cul 3E **5**
Hewitt St. WA4: Warr 2E **33**
Heyes, The WA7: Run 6E **41**
Heyes Dr. WA13: Lymm 3A **36**
Heyes Mt. L35: R'hill 1E **15**
Heyes Rd. WA8: Wid 5E **27**
Hey Lock Cl. WA12: New W 1G **7**
Heysham Cl. WA7: Murd 3A **52**
Hey Wood Cl. WA12: New W 1G **7**
Heywood Gdns. L35: Whis 1A **14**
Hibbert St. WA8: Wid 5B **28**
Hickory Cl. WA1: W'ston 4E **23**
Higham Av. WA5: Warr 2B **20**
Highbank Cl. M44: Cad 3H **13**
Highbank Rd. WA6: K'ley 5H **57**
Higher Ashton WA8: Wid 2H **27**
Higher Heyes Dr. WA6: K'ley . . .6H **57**
Higher Heys WA7: Beech 4F **51**
Higher Knutsford Rd.
WA4: S Hth 2H **33**
Higher La.
WA4: Dutt, Lwr Wh 6F **53**
WA13: Lymm 3C **36**
Higher Rd. L26: Halew 2A **38**
HIGHER RUNCORN **6H 39**
HIGHER WALTON **6A 32**
Highfield CH2: Elt 1F **59**
Highfield Av. WA4: App 3F **45**
WA5: Gt San 6E **19**
Highfield Cres. WA8: Wid 3A **28**
Highfield Dr. WA13: Lymm 3A **36**
Highfield La. WA2: Win 1E **9**
Highfield Rd. WA8: Wid 4H **27**
WA13: Lymm 2A **36**
Highgate Cl. WA7: Nort 6B **42**
High Gates Cl. WA5: Warr 4A **20**
High Gates Lodge WA5: Warr . . .4A **20**
Highlands Rd. WA7: Run 6H **39**
High Legh Rd. WA13: Lymm 5G **37**
High St. L24: Hale 6B **48**
WA6: Frod 3B **56**
WA7: Run 5A **40**
High Vw. WA6: Hel 1E **61**
High Warren Cl. WA4: App 2D **44**
Highwood Rd. WA4: App 6E **33**
Hilary Cl. WA5: Gt San 5B **18**
WA8: Wid 2E **29**
Hilden Pl. WA2: Warr 3F **21**
Hilden Rd. WA2: P'gate 2G **21**
Hillberry Cres. WA4: Warr 2D **32**
HILLCLIFFE **6E 33**
Hill Cliffe Rd. WA4: Walt 5D **32**
Hillcrest WA7: Run 6D **40**
Hillfield WA6: Frod 4B **56**
WA7: Nort 1B **52**
Hillfoot Cres. WA4: S Hth 6D **32**
Hillock La. WA1: W'ston 4B **22**
Hill Rd. Nth. WA6: Hel 2E **61**
Hill Rd. Sth. WA6: Hel 2E **61**
Hillsboro Av. WA6: Frod 4C **56**
Hillside WA13: Lymm 4H **37**
Hillside Av. WA7: Run 1G **49**
Hillside Cl. WA6: Hel 1F **61**
Hillside Gro. WA5: Penk 1D **30**
Hillside Rd. WA4: App 3E **45**
WA6: Frod 4C **56**
Hill St. WA1: Warr 6D **20**
WA7: Run 5A **40**
Hilltop WA7: Nort 2A **52**
Hill Top Rd. WA4: Pres H 3D **52**
WA4: S Hth 3H **33**
Hilltop Rd. WA1: W'ston 3C **22**
WA13: Lymm 3A **36**
Hill Vw. WA8: Wid 6H **15**
Hill Vw. Av. WA6: Hel 4C **60**
Hillview Cl. WA6: Frod 4C **56**
Hilton Av. WA5: Gt San 6F **19**
Hilton Dr. M44: Cad 4G **13**
Hindle Av. WA5: Warr 2B **20**
Hinton Cres. WA4: App 5G **33**
Hinton Rd. WA7: Run 6A **40**
Hitchens Cl. WA7: Murd 2B **52**
HMP Risley WA3: Ris 1E **11**
HM Young Offenders
Institution Thorn Cross
WA4: App T 3C **46**
Hobb La. WA4: Dares, Moore . . .2G **43**
Hobby Ct. WA7: Pal F 3E **51**
Hob Hey La. WA3: Cul 3D **4**
Hob La. CH2: Wim T 6E **59**
WA6: Dun H 6D **58**
Hodgkinson Av. WA5: Warr 2B **20**
Hoghton Rd. L24: Hale 5A **3**
Holbeck WA7: Nort 2A **5**
Holborn Ct. WA8: Wid 2H **2**
Holbrook Cl. WA5: Gt San 5C **1**
Holcroft Grange WA3: Cul 4E
Holcroft La. WA3: Cul . . .4H **5** & 1C **1**
Holes La. WA1: W'ston 3B **2**
Holford Av. WA5: Warr 3B **2**
Holford Moss WA7: Nort 4B **4**
Holkham Cl. WA8: Wid 4H **2**
Holland St. WA5: Warr 6A **2**
Hollies, The WA7: Run 1D **5**
HOLLINFARE **6F 1**
Hollins Dr. WA2: Win 3C
HOLLINS GREEN **1E 2**
Hollins La. WA2: Win 3A
HOLLINS PARK HOSPITAL **3B**
Hollins Way WA8: Hale B 2D **3**
Holloway WA7: Run 6H **3**
Hollow Dr. WA4: S Hth 4G **3**
Hollow La. WA6: K'ley 5G **5**
Holly Bank WA6: Alv 3F **6**
WA6: Frod 3C **5**
WA13: Lymm 3B **3**
Hollybank WA4: Moore 2E **4**
Hollybank Cvn. Pk. WA3: Rix . . .2E **2**
Hollybank Ct. WA8: Wid 4H **2**
Hollybank Rd. WA7: Halt 6F **4**
Holly Bush La. WA3: Rix 3A **2**
Holly Cl. L24: Hale 5B **4**
Holly Ct. WA6: Hel 6E **5**
Holly Farm Ct. WA8: Wid 1H **2**
Holly Gro. WA1: P'ton 4A **2**
Hollyhedge La. WA4: H Walt . . .1H **4**
Holly Rd. WA5: Penk 6C **1**
WA13: Lymm 6F **2**
Holly Ter. WA5: Penk 6D **1**
Holly Wlk. M31: Part 6H **1**
Holm Dr. CH2: Elt 2G **5**
Holmes Ct. WA3: Bchwd 5C **1**
Holmesfield Rd. WA1: Warr 6F **2**
Holmfield CH2: Elt 2G **5**
Holmfield Av. WA7: Run 5C **4**
Holt La. WA7: Halt 1F **5**
Holyhead Cl. WA5: Call 6H
Holyrood Av. WA8: Wid 1A **2**
Holywell Dr. WA1: Warr 6E **2**
Homeway WA6: Hel 3D **6**
Honeysuckle Cl. WA8: Wid 1B **2**
Honister Av. WA2: Warr 1E **21**
Honister Gro. WA7: Beech 4E **5**
Honiton Way WA5: Penk 1C **3**
Hood La. WA5: Gt San 6G **1**
Hood La. Nth. WA5: Gt San 5G **1**
Hood Mnr. Cen. WA5: Gt San . . .5G **1**
Hood Rd. WA8: Wid 4H **2**
Hoolpool La. WA6: Elt 6B **5**
Hopefield Rd. WA13: Lymm 1F **3**
Hopwood St. WA1: Warr 5E **2**
(not continuous
Hornbeam Cl. WA7: Wind H 6A **4**
Hornby La. WA2: Win 3C
Horrocks La. WA1: Warr 6D **2**
Horsemarket St. WA1: Warr 6D **2**
Horseshoe Cl. WA6: K'ley 5G **5**
Horseshoe Cres.
WA2: Warr 6G
Hoscar Ct. WA8: Wid 6F **2**
Hospital Way WA7: Pal F 2F **5**
Hostock Cl. L35: Whis 1A **1**
HOUGH GREEN **4C 2**
Hough Grn. Rd. WA8: Wid 3C **2**
Hough Green Station (Rail) . . .**3D 2**
Hough's La. WA4: H Walt 2C **44**
Houghton Cl. WA8: Wid 3C **2**
Houghton Cft. WA8: Cron 6E **1**
HOUGHTON GREEN **5G**
Houghton Rd. L24: Hale 6A **3**
Houghton St. WA2: Warr 5D **2**
WA8: Wid 3D **2**
House La. WA8: Wid 6H **2**
Houston Gdns. WA5: Gt San 3E **1**
Hove, The WA7: Murd 3B **5**
(not continuous
Howard Av. WA13: Lymm 1E **3**
Howard Ct. WA7: Mnr P 3A **4**
Howard Rd. WA3: Cul 5G
Howarth Ct. WA7: Run 5B **4**
Howey La. WA6: Frod 4A **5**
Howey Ri. WA6: Frod 4A **5**
HOWLEY **6E 21**
Howley La. WA1: Warr 6F **2**
Howley Quay WA1: Warr 6F **2**

Howley Quay Ind. Est.—Lee Ct.

owley Quay Ind. Est.
WA1: Warr 6F 21
owson Rd. WA2: Warr 1E 21
oylake Cl. WA7: Murd 2A 52
(not continuous)
oyle St. WA5: Warr 4B 20
udson Cl. WA5: Old H 3H 19
ughes Av. WA2: Warr 1F 21
ughes Pl. WA2: Warr 1F 21
ughes St. WA4: Warr 2E 33
ULME 6D 8
umber Cl. WA8: Wid 2F 29
umber Rd. WA2: Warr 1G 21
ume St. WA1: Warr 5F 21
umphrey's Cl. WA7: Murd 2B 52
unt Cl. WA5: Gt San 3F 19
unter Av. WA2: Warr 1D 20
unters Ct. WA6: Hel 1F 61
WA7: Pal F 3E 51
unters Hill WA6: K'ley 6H 57
untley St. WA5: Gt San 1G 31
unts Fld. Cl. WA13: Lymm 3B 36
unts La. WA4: S Hth 3H 33
urley Cl. WA5: Gt San 6G 19
urst, The WA6: K'ley 5H 57
urst La. WA3: G'bury 1H 5
urst Mill La. WA3: G'bury 5H 5
urst St. WA8: Wid 3A 40
utchinson St. WA8: Wid 1H 39
utton Cl. WA3: Cul 2E 5
yde Cl. WA7: Beech 3D 50

I

bis Ct. WA1: Warr 2C 32
lex Av. WA2: Win 3D 8
nce & Elton Station (Rail) 1F 59
nce La. CH2: Elt 1F 59
CH2: Wim T 6D 58
nce Orchards CH2: Elt 1F 59
ngham Rd. WA8: Wid 1H 27
ngham's Rd. WA3: Croft 6A 4
nglenook Rd. WA5: Penk 1D 30
ngleton Gro. WA7: Beech 4D 50
nglewood Cl. WA3: Bchwd 3H 11
nner Gosling Cl. WA4: Hatt 6B 44
nsall Rd. WA2: P'gate 1H 21
ntack La. WA16: H Legh 3G 47
(not continuous)
nternational Bus. Cen.
WA5: W'brk 1G 19
reland Rd. L24: Hale 6A 38
(not continuous)
reland St. WA2: Warr 3D 20
WA8: Wid 3D 28
ris Cl. WA8: Wid 3E 27
rlam Ind. Est. M44: Irlam 2H 13
rwell La. WA7: Run 4B 40
rwell Rd. WA4: Warr 3D 32
rwell St. WA8: Wid 3A 40
sherwood Cl. WA2: Fearn 6H 9
slington Grn. WA8: Wid 1D 28
veagh Cl. WA7: Pal F 2G 51
ver Cl. WA8: Cron 5E 15
vychurch M. WA7: Run 5D 40
vy Farm Ct. L24: Hale 6B 48
vy Farm Gdns. WA3: Cul 3D 4
vy Rd. WA1: W'ston 4E 23
vy St. WA7: Run 6A 40
vy Wlk. M31: Part 6H 13

J

ackies La. WA13: Lymm 1D 36
(not continuous)
Jackson Av. WA1: P'ton 4H 21
WA3: Cul 4E 5
Jackson Cl. L35: R'hill 2F 15
Jackson St. WA5: B'wood 3C 6
James Cl. WA8: Wid 3A 40
James St. WA1: Warr 6D 20
Jasmine Gro. WA8: Wid 5F 27
Jay Cl. WA3: Bchwd 5G 11
Jay's Cl. WA7: Murd 2C 52
Jellicoe Av. M44: Cad 3H 13
Jensen Ct. WA7: Ast 4C 40
Jervis Cl. WA2: Fearn 6A 10
Jockey St. WA2: Warr 4D 20
John Middleton Cl. L24: Hale 6A 38
John Rd. WA13: Lymm 2A 36
Johns Av. WA7: Run 6H 39
Johnson's La. WA8: Wid 4E 29
John St. M44: Cad 4H 13
WA2: Warr 5D 20
Joseph St. WA8: Wid 3C 28
Joule St. WA3: Ris 4F 11
Joy La. WA5: B'wood 5B 6
WA9: Clock F 1E 17
Joy Wlk. WA9: Clock F 1E 17
Jubilee Av. WA1: P'gate 3H 21
WA5: Penk 1C 30
Jubilee Dr. L35: Whis 1A 14
Jubilee Gro. WA13: Lymm 1A 36
Jubilee Way WA8: Wid 4G 27
Jubits La. WA8: Bold H 3A 16
WA9: Sut M 3A 16
Julian Way WA8: Wid 1H 27
Juniper La. WA3: W'ston 3G 23
Jurby Ct. WA2: P'gate 2H 21

K

Kansas Pl. WA5: Gt San 4F 19
Karen Cl. WA5: B'wood 3D 6
Kaye Av. WA3: Cul 4F 5
Kay La. WA13: Lymm 5F 37
Keats Cl. WA8: Wid 5H 27
Keats Gro. WA2: Warr 1E 21
Keble St. WA8: Wid 6B 28
KECKWICK 3D 42
Keckwick La. WA4: Dares 3D 42
Keeper's Rd. WA4: Grap 6A 34
Keepers Wlk. WA7: Cas 5F 41
Keith Av. WA5: Gt San 5B 18
Kelburn Ct. WA3: Ris 3F 11
Kelsall Cl. WA3: Bchwd 6C 10
WA8: Wid 3F 27
Kelvin Cl. WA3: Ris 3D 10
Kelvin St. WA3: Ris 3E 11
Kemberton Dr. WA8: Wid 6A 16
Kemmel Av. WA4: Warr 3E 33
Kempton Cl. WA7: Run 3C 50
Kendal Av. WA2: Warr 1E 21
Kendal Ri. WA7: Beech 4D 50
Kendal Rd. WA8: Wid 4E 27
Kendrick St. WA1: Warr 6C 20
Kenilworth Av. WA7: Run 1B 50
Kenilworth Dr. WA1: P'gate 3H 21
Kenley Av. WA8: Cron 6F 15
Kenmore Gro. M44: Cad 3H 13
Kenneth Rd. WA8: Wid 5E 27
Kennington Pk. WA8: Wid 2G 27
Kensington Av. WA4: Grap 3C 34
Kensington Cl. WA8: Wid 1D 28
Kent Gro. WA7: Run 6B 40
Kentmere Pl. WA2: Warr 6C 8
Kent Rd. M31: Part 1H 25
M44: Cad 4G 13
WA5: Gt San 1G 31
Kent St. WA4: Warr 1E 33
WA8: Wid 4B 28
Kenview Cl. WA8: Hale B 2C 38
KENYON 3A 4
Kenyon Av. WA5: Penk 6C 18
Kenyon La. WA3: Croft 2A 4
WA3: Low 2A 4
Kerfoot Bus. Pk. WA2: Warr 3C 20
(Kerfoot St.)
WA2: Warr 4C 20
(Side Kerfoot St.)
Kerfoot St. WA2: Warr 4C 20
Kershaw St. WA8: Wid 4F 27
Kestrel La. WA3: Bchwd 5E 11
Kestrels Way WA7: Pal F 3F 51
Keswick Av. WA2: Warr 1E 21
Keswick Cl. M44: Cad 4H 13
WA8: Wid 4E 27
Keswick Cres. WA2: Warr 1E 21
Keswick Dr. WA6: Frod 3C 56
Kew Gdns. Cl. WA8: Wid 1D 28
Keyes Cl. WA3: Bchwd 5F 11
Keyes Gdns. WA3: Bchwd 5F 11
Kildare Cl. L24: Hale 5B 48
Kildonan Rd. WA4: Grap 3A 34
Kilford Cl. WA5: Call 1A 20
Killingworth La.
WA3: Bchwd 4G 11
Kilncroft WA7: Brook 4H 51
(not continuous)
Kilsby Dr. WA8: Wid 3E 29
Kilshaw Rd. WA5: B'wood 3D 6
Kilsyth Cl. WA2: Fearn 5H 9
Kimberley Dr. WA4: S Hth 4E 33
Kimberley St. WA5: Warr 6A 20
King Arthurs Wlk. WA7: Cas 1G 51
King Edward St. WA1: Warr 4G 21
Kingfisher Cl. WA3: Bchwd 5F 11
WA7: Beech 4F 51
King George Cres.
WA1: Warr 4G 21
Kingham Cl. WA8: Wid 4D 28
King James Ct. WA7: Pal F 3E 51
Kingsbury Cl. WA4: App 4F 45
Kingsbury Rd. WA8: Wid 1D 28
Kings Ct. WA7: Mnr P 3B 42
Kingsdale Av. L35: R'hill 1F 15
Kingsdale Rd. WA5: Gt San 3D 18
Kings Dr. WA6: Hel 2D 60
Kingshead Cl. WA7: Cas 5G 41
Kingsland Grange
WA1: W'ston 2C 22
KINGSLEY 5H 57
Kingsley Cres. WA7: Run 6A 40
Kingsley Dr. WA4: App 6E 33
Kingsley Grn. WA6: Frod 6E 57
Kingsley Rd. WA6: Frod 5D 56
WA7: Run 6A 40
Kingsmead Ct. WA3: Croft 1A 10
Kings Mdw. WA7: Nort 1A 52
Kings M. WA4: S Hth 5E 33
Kingsnorth L35: Whis 1B 14
Kings Rd. WA2: Fearn 1A 22
Kingston Av. WA5: Gt San 5C 18
Kingston Cl. WA7: Run 5E 41
King St. WA7: Run 4A 40
Kingsway WA6: Frod 3B 56
WA8: Wid 6A 28
Kingsway Ho. *WA4: Westy* *1H 33*
(off Kingsway Sth.)
WA8: Wid 6A 28
Kingsway Leisure Cen. 5A 28
Kingsway Nth. WA1: Warr 5G 21
Kingsway Sth. WA1: Warr 6G 21
WA4: Westy 2H 33
KINGSWOOD 1F 19
Kingswood Grn. WA5: W'brk 1F 19
Kingswood Rd. WA5: W'brk 1E 19
Kinnock Pk. WA5: B'wood 3C 6
Kinross Cl. WA2: Fearn 5H 9
Kinsale Dr. WA3: Bchwd 5C 10
Kintore Dr. WA5: Gt San 5B 18
Kipling Av. WA2: Warr 2E 21
Kipling Cres. WA8: Wid 4H 27
Kirkacre Av. WA12: New W 1G 7
Kirkby Rd. WA3: Cul 4F 5
Kirkcaldy Av. WA5: Gt San 5B 18
Kirkham Cl. WA5: Gt San 1F 31
Kirkham Rd. WA8: Wid 3C 28
Kirkstone Av. WA2: Warr 1E 21
Kirkstone Cres. WA7: Beech 5G 51
Kirkwall Dr. WA5: Penk 2E 31
Kitchener Av. M44: Cad 5G 13
Knight Rd. WA5: B'wood 3D 6
Knightsbridge Av. WA4: Grap 2C 34
Knightsbridge Cl. WA8: Wid 1D 28
Knightsbridge Ct. WA1: Warr 6C 20
Knoll, The WA7: Pal F 2F 51
Knowles St. WA8: Wid 3C 28
Knowsley Expressway
WA8: Wid 1A 26
Knowsley Rd. L35: R'hill 1F 15
Knutsford Old Rd. WA4: Grap 3A 34
Knutsford Rd. WA4: Grap 3A 34
WA4: Warr 1E 33

L

LA Bowl 6C 8
Laburnum Av. WA1: W'ston 4C 22
Laburnum Ct. WA13: Lymm 1F 37
Laburnum Gro. WA7: Run 1B 50
Laburnum La. WA5: Gt San 5A 18
Laburnum Rd. M44: Cad 4H 13
Lacey Ct. WA8: Wid 6A 28
Lacey St. WA8: Wid 6A 28
Ladies Wlk. WA8: Bold H 1G 17
WA9: Bold 1G 17
WA2: Win 3B 8
Lady Acre Cl. WA13: Lymm 3B 36
Ladycroft Cl. WA1: W'ston 4E 23
Lady La. WA3: Croft 6C 4
Ladypool L24: Hale 5A 48
Lady Richeld Cl. WA7: Nort 4B 42
Ladywood Rd. WA5: Old H 2G 19
Laira Ct. WA2: Warr 4E 21
Laira St. WA2: Warr 4E 21
Lakeside Cl. WA8: Wid 5C 26
Lakeside Dr. WA1: Warr 2C 32
Lakeside Rd. WA13: Lymm 4B 36
Lake Vw. L35: Whis 3A 14
Laleston Cl. WA8: Wid 5G 27
Lambourn Av. WA8: Cron 6E 15
Lambsickle Cl. WA7: West 3H 49
Lambsickle La.
WA7: Run, West 3H 49
(not continuous)
Lambs La. WA1: P'ton 4A 22
WA1: P'ton, P'gate 3A 22
Lamerton Cl. WA5: Penk 1B 30
Lampeter Cl. WA5: Call 1H 19
Lamport Cl. WA8: Wid 2E 29
Lancashire Rd. M31: Part 1H 25
Lancaster Av. WA7: Run 1G 49
WA8: Wid 3C 26
Lancaster Cl. WA2: P'gate 1H 21
Lancaster Ct. WA4: S Hth 4G 33
Lancaster Rd. M44: Cad 4G 13
WA8: Wid 2A 28
Lancaster St. WA5: Warr 6A 20
Lancer Ct. WA7: Ast 4E 41
Lancing Av. WA2: Warr 6C 8
Landcut La. WA3: Bchwd 6D 10
Lander Cl. WA5: Old H 4H 19
Landscape Dene WA6: Hel 1F 61
Landseer Av. WA4: Warr 4D 32
Langbar L35: Whis 1A 14
Langcliffe Cl. WA3: Cul 4E 5
Langdale Av. WA13: Lymm 2D 36
Langdale Cl. WA2: Warr 6G 9
WA8: Wid 5E 27
Langdale Rd. WA7: Run 5B 40
Langdale Way WA6: Frod 2C 56
Langden Cl. WA3: Cul 3D 4
Langford L24: Hale 5A 48
Langford Way WA4: App T 3D 46
Langland Cl. WA5: Call 1A 20
Langton Cl. WA8: Wid 2D 26
Langton Grn. WA1: W'ston 4D 22
Langwell Cl. WA3: Bchwd 4G 11
Lansdowne WA3: Cul 5E 5
WA6: Frod 5D 56
Lapwing Gro. WA7: Pal F 3G 51
Lapwing La. WA4: Moore 6D 30
Larch Av. WA5: Penk 6C 18
WA8: Wid 3B 28
Larch Cl. WA7: Run 2C 50
Larch Rd. M31: Part 6H 13
WA7: Run 2C 50
Larchways WA4: App 2F 45
Larkfield Av. WA1: P'ton 4A 22
Larkspur Cl. WA7: Beech 5F 51
Larkstoke Cl. WA4: App 1G 45
Larne Way WA8: Wid 2G 27
Laser Quest 5D 20
Laskey La. WA4: Thel 1F 35
LATCHFORD 2F 33
Latchford St. WA4: Westy 2A 34
Latham Av. WA6: Hel 4D 60
WA7: Run 5B 40
Lathom Av. WA2: Warr 3D 20
Launceston Cl. WA7: Brook 3A 52
Launceston Dr. WA5: Penk 2C 30
Laurel Av. WA1: W'ston 4D 22
Laurel Bank WA4: Grap 4C 34
WA8: Wid 2A 28
Laurel Farm Ct. CH2: Elt 1F 59
Laurel Wlk. M31: Part 1H 25
(not continuous)
Lavender Cl. WA7: Run 6C 40
Lavender Wlk. M31: Part 1H 25
Lawn Av. WA1: P'gate 3H 21
Lawnswood Gro. CH2: Elt 2F 59
Lawson Cl. WA1: W'ston 4E 23
Lawton Cl. WA3: Cul 4E 5
Lawton Rd. L35: R'hill 1F 15
Laxey Av. WA1: W'ston 5D 22
Layland Av. WA3: Cul 3E 5
Layton Cl. WA3: Bchwd 6E 11
Leacroft Rd. WA3: Ris 3F 11
Lea Cross Gro. WA8: Wid 2E 27
Leamington Cl. WA5: Gt San 3E 19
Leaside WA7: Run 6D 40
Leatham Cl. WA3: Bchwd 6E 11
Ledsham Cl. WA3: Bchwd 6C 10
Ledston Cl. WA7: Wind H 6B 42
Ledyard Cl. WA5: Old H 4H 19
Lee Cl. L35: R'hill 2F 15
Lee Ct. WA2: Warr 1E 21

A-Z Warrington 71

Lee Rd. WA5: Gt San	5F 19
Lees, The WA5: Gt San	3E 19
(not continuous)	
Legh St. WA1: Warr	6C 20
WA13: Lymm	2C 36
Leicester St. WA5: Warr	6A 20
(not continuous)	
Leigh Av. WA8: Wid	4H 27
Leigh Grn. Cl. WA8: Wid	5E 27
Leinster Gdns. WA7: Run	4H 39
Leinster St. WA7: Run	4H 39
Leonard St. WA2: Warr	4E 21
WA4: S Hth	4E 33
WA7: West P	2F 49
Leon Cl. WA5: Gt San	4B 18
Lessingham Rd. WA8: Wid	2H 27
Levens Cl. WA5: Warr	5B 20
Levens Way WA8: Wid	5E 27
Levisham Gdns. WA5: Warr	4A 20
Lewis Av. WA5: Warr	1B 20
Lewis Cres. WA8: Wid	6A 28
Lewis Gro. WA8: Wid	4F 27
Lexden St. WA5: Warr	5A 20
Leyton Cl. WA7: Run	3B 50
Libson Cl. WA2: Fearn	6A 10
Lichfield Av. WA4: Grap	6A 34
Lickers La. L35: Whis	1A 14
Lightburn St. WA7: Run	6H 39
Lighthouse Rd. L24: Hale	3A 48
Lilac Av. WA5: Gt San	6E 19
WA8: Wid	3B 28
Lilac Cres. WA7: Run	1C 50
Lilac Gro. WA4: S Hth	4G 33
Lilford Av. WA5: Warr	3A 20
Lilford Dr. WA5: Gt San	5D 18
Lilford St. WA5: Warr	4B 20
(not continuous)	
Lime Av. WA6: Frod	3C 56
WA8: Wid	3B 28
Lime Cl. WA3: Rix	1E 25
Limefield Av. WA13: Lymm	3D 36
Lime Gro. CH2: Elt	2E 59
WA7: Run	1C 50
Limekiln La. WA5: B'wood	6C 6
Limekiln Row WA7: Cas	1G 51
Limerick Cl. WA8: Wid	2G 27
Limes, The WA3: Cul	3D 4
Lime Tree Av. WA5: S Hth	4G 33
Limetree Av. WA1: P'gate	3H 21
Limetree La. WA16: H Legh	6H 37
Lime Wlk. M31: Part	6H 13
Linacre La. WA8: Wid	6G 15
Lincoln Av. M44: Cad	5G 13
Lincoln Cl. WA1: W'ston	5E 23
WA7: Run	3C 50
Lincoln Ct. WA6: Hel	2D 60
Lincoln Sq. WA8: Wid	3B 28
Lincoln Way L35: R'hill	2F 15
Linden Cl. WA1: W'ston	4D 22
WA13: Lymm	1D 36
Linden Ct. WA8: Wid	1H 27
Linden Dr. WA6: Hel	6D 60
Linden Gro. M44: Cad	4H 13
Linden Way WA8: Wid	1H 27
Lindfield Cl. WA4: Moore	2F 43
Lindi Av. WA4: Grap	4B 34
Lindisfarne Ct. WA8: Wid	5H 15
Lindley Av. WA4: Westy	1H 33
Lindsworth Cl. WA5: Gt San	5G 19
Linear Vw. WA12: New W	1G 7
Lingfield Rd. WA7: Run	6G 39
LINGLEY GREEN	4B 18
Lingley Grn. Av.	
WA5: Gt San	5A 18
Lingley Mere Bus. Pk.	
WA5: Gt San	3B 18
Lingley Rd. WA5: Gt San	5B 18
Lingwell Av. WA8: Wid	3F 27
Lingwood Rd. WA5: Gt San	5D 18
Links, The WA3: Ris	3D 10
Linkside Av. WA2: Win	3D 8
Link Wlk. M31: Part	1H 25
Linkway WA7: Run	1C 50
Linnet Cl. WA2: Warr	6F 9
Linnet Gro. WA3: Bchwd	6E 11
Linnets Pk. WA7: Run	6B 40
Linwood Cl. WA7: Brook	4A 52
Linwood Gro. L35: Whis	1A 14
Liskeard Cl. WA7: Brook	3H 51
Lister Rd. WA7: Ast	4C 40
Littlebourne WA7: Murd	2C 52
Littlecote Gdns. WA4: App	3F 45

Littledale Rd. WA5: Gt San	4D 18
Littlegate WA7: Run	1E 51
Littlestone Cl. WA8: Wid	1A 28
Littleton Cl. WA5: Gt San	1H 31
LITTLE TOWN	6C 4
Littlewood Cl. L35: Whis	1A 14
Littondale Av. L35: R'hill	1F 15
Liverpool Pl. WA8: Wid	4E 27
Liverpool Rd. M44: Cad	6G 13
WA1: Warr	6B 20
WA3: G'brk	6G 13
WA5: Gt San	5A 18
WA5: Warr	6B 20
WA8: Wid	4D 26
Liverpool Row WA12: New W	1H 7
Livingstone Cl. WA5: Old H	4H 19
Lobelia Gro. WA7: Beech	5F 51
Local Cen. WA7: Cas	5G 41
Loch St. WA7: Run	4A 40
(not continuous)	
Locker Av. WA2: Warr	1D 20
Lockerbie Cl. WA2: Warr	6G 9
Lockett Rd. WA8: Wid	2A 28
Lockett St. WA4: Latch	2H 33
Lockgate E. WA7: Wind H	5A 42
Lockgate W. WA7: Wind H	5H 41
LOCKING STUMPS	4C 10
Locking Stumps Cen.	
WA3: Bchwd	5D 10
Locking Stumps La.	
WA2: Bchwd, Fearn	6B 10
WA3: Bchwd	6B 10
Lock La. M31: Part	6H 13
Lock Rd. WA1: P'ton	5H 21
Lockton La. WA5: Warr	4A 20
Lockwood Vw. WA7: Pres B	4D 52
Lodge Cl. WA13: Lymm	1F 37
Lodge Dr. WA3: Cul	4F 5
Lodge Hollow WA6: Hel	1D 60
Lodge La. WA5: Warr	4A 20
WA7: Halt	1E 51
WA8: Cron	1C 26
Lodge Rd. WA8: Wid	5D 26
Lofthouse Ga. WA8: Wid	2H 27
London Rd.	
WA4: App, S Hth, Thel	4E 33
WA6: Frod	3B 56
London Row WA12: New W	1H 7
Longbarn Blvd. WA2: Bchwd	1C 22
Long Barn La. WA1: W'ston	2D 22
WA2: Fearn	1B 22
WA2: P'gate	1C 22
(not continuous)	
Longbenton Way	
WA7: Mnr P	3H 41
Longbutt La. WA13: Lymm	2D 36
(not continuous)	
Longdin St. WA4: Westy	2G 33
Longfield Gdns. M44: Cad	5H 13
Longfield Rd. WA2: Warr	2E 21
LONGFORD	2D 20
Longford Dr. WA8: Wid	3G 27
Longford St. WA2: Warr	4D 20
Long Hey L35: Whis	2A 14
Long La. WA2: Warr	2D 20
Longleat Cl. WA5: Warr	4B 20
Longshaw St. WA5: Warr	1B 20
Long Spinney WA7: Nort	1A 52
Longster Cl. WA6: Hel	3D 60
Long Wlk. M31: Part	6H 13
Longwood Rd. WA4: App	1G 45
Lonsdale Cl. WA5: Gt San	3C 18
WA8: Wid	4E 27
Looe Cl. WA8: Wid	3G 27
Lord Nelson St. WA1: Warr	6E 21
Lordship La. WA6: Frod	5B 54
Lords Cl. WA3: Bchwd	5C 10
Lords St. M44: Cad	3G 13
Lord St. WA3: Croft	1A 10
WA4: Warr	1D 32
WA7: Run	4H 39
Lostock Av. WA5: Warr	3B 20
Loushers La.	
WA4: Latch, Warr	3E 33
Lovage Cl. WA2: P'gate	1C 22
Lovel Ter. WA8: Hale B	2D 38
Lovely La. WA5: Warr	5A 20
Lowe Av. WA4: Westy	1H 33
Lwr. Appleton Rd. WA8: Wid	4B 28
Lwr. Church St. WA8: Wid	2A 40
Lwr. Hill Top Rd. WA4: S Hth	3H 33
Lwr. House La. WA8: Wid	6H 27
LOWER IRLAM	1H 13

Lwr. Rake La. WA6: Hel	1D 60
Lower Rd. WA8: Hale B	1A 38
Lwr. Robin Hood La.	
WA6: Hel	2C 60
LOWER STRETTON	6G 45
LOWER WALTON	5D 32
Lwr. Wash La. WA4: Westy	2G 33
Loweswater Cl. WA2: Warr	6D 8
Lowfield Gdns. WA3: G'bury	6H 5
Lowlands Rd. WA7: Run	5H 39
Lowry Cl. WA5: Gt San	5H 19
Lowther Av. WA3: Cul	3F 5
Lowther Dr. L35: R'hill	1D 14
LOWTON ST MARY'S	1A 4
Loxley Cl. WA5: Gt San	3E 19
Loyola Hey L35: R'hill	3G 15
Ludlow Cl. WA1: P'gate	2B 22
Ludlow Cres. WA7: Run	1B 50
LUGSDALE	6C 28
(not continuous)	
Lugsdale Rd. WA8: Wid	6B 28
Lumb Brook M. WA4: S Hth	4G 33
Lumb Brook Rd. WA4: App	5G 33
(not continuous)	
Lumber La. WA5: B'wood	1C 6
Lumbrook Rd.	
WA4: App, App T	1A 46
Lumley Wlk. L24: Hale	6A 38
Luneway WA8: Wid	4E 27
LUNTS HEATH	1B 28
Lunt's Heath Rd. WA8: Wid	6A 16
Luton St. WA4: App	6A 28
Lychgate WA4: H Walt	6B 32
Lycroft Cl. WA7: Run	3B 50
Lydbury Cl. WA5: Call	1H 19
Lydiate La. WA7: West P	2F 49
Lydstep Ct. WA5: Call	1A 20
Lyme Gro. WA13: Lymm	3A 36
Lyme St. WA1: Warr	6D 20
Lyme Tree Ct. WA8: Cron	5E 15
LYMM	2B 36
Lymm Bri. WA13: Lymm	2C 36
Lymmhay La. WA13: Lymm	1C 36
Lymmington Av.	
WA13: Lymm	2A 36
Lymm Leisure Cen.	3E 37
Lyncastle Rd. WA4: App T	4D 46
Lyncastle Way WA4: App T	3D 46
Lyndale Rd. WA7: Run	1C 50
Lyndale Av. WA2: Fearn	1H 21
WA2: Warr	3F 21
Lyndon Gro. WA7: Run	1B 50
Lyneham L35: Whis	1A 14
Lynham Av. WA5: Gt San	6F 19
Lynton Av. WA7: Run	2C 50
Lynthorpe Av. M44: Cad	3H 13
Lynton Cres. WA8: Wid	3G 27
Lynton Gdns. WA4: App	3F 45
Lynton Grn. WA8: Wid	3G 27
Lynwood Av. WA4: App	6E 33
Lyon Ct. WA4: Latch	2H 33
Lyons La. WA4: App	1F 45
Lyons Rd. WA5: Penk	1D 30
Lyon St. WA4: Latch	2H 33
Lyster Cl. WA3: Bchwd	6F 11
Lytham Cl. WA5: Gt San	2E 31
Lytham Ho. WA3: Ris	3D 10
Lytham Rd. WA8: Wid	3B 28
Lytherton Av. M44: Cad	5G 13
Lythgoes La. WA2: Warr	5D 20

M

MacArthur Rd. WA5: Gt San	5F 19
McCarthy Cl. WA3: Bchwd	5G 11
McClellan Pl. WA8: Wid	4B 28
Macdermott Rd. WA8: Wid	2A 40
McKee Av. WA2: Warr	1D 20
McKinley Way WA8: Wid	2H 27
Madeleine McKenna Ct.	
WA8: Wid	2D 26
Magenta Av. M44: Irlam	3H 13
Mag La. WA13: Lymm	6D 36
WA16: H Legh, Lymm	6D 36
Magnolia Cl. WA1: W'ston	4E 23
Magnolia Dr. WA7: Beech	5F 51
Main Dr. L35: Whis	2A 14
Main Front L35: Whis	2A 14
Main La. WA3: Croft	3A 4
Main St. WA6: Frod	3A 56
WA7: Halt	6F 41
Mairesfield Av. WA4: Grap	3B 34

Major Cross St. WA8: Wid	6A 28
Malahide Cl. WA8: Wid	2F 27
Malcolm Av. WA2: Warr	2F 21
Malcolm St. WA7: Run	5B 40
Malham Cl. WA5: Gt San	3C 18
Malhamdale Av. L35: R'hill	1F 15
Malin Cl. L24: Hale	5B 48
Maliston Rd. WA5: Gt San	6F 19
Mall, The WA1: Warr	6D 20
Mallard Cl. WA2: Warr	6F 9
WA7: Beech	4F 51
Mallard La. WA3: Bchwd	6F 11
Malmesbury Pk. WA7: Nort	5B 42
Malpas Dr. WA5: Gt San	6G 19
Malpas Rd. WA7: Run	2B 50
Malpas Way WA5: Gt San	1G 31
Maltmans Rd. WA13: Lymm	2B 36
Malton Cl. WA8: Cron	6E 15
Malvern Cl. WA5: Gt San	3E 19
Manchester Rd.	
WA1: P'ton, Warr, W'ston	
	5E 21
WA3: Rix, W'ston	4G 23
Manchester Row	
WA12: New W	1H 7
Mancroft Cl. WA1: W'ston	4E 23
Mandarin Cl. WA1: Warr	2C 32
Manley Gdns. WA5: Warr	6B 20
Manley Rd. WA6: Alv, Manl	5F 61
WA6: Frod	6C 56
Manley Vw. CH2: Elt	2G 59
Manna Dr. CH2: Elt	2G 59
Manor Av. L35: R'hill	1E 15
Manor Cl. WA1: W'ston	4D 22
WA13: Lymm	3C 36
Manor Farm Ct. WA6: Frod	2C 56
Mnr. Farm M. WA7: Mnr P	3B 42
Mnr. Farm Rd. WA7: Mnr P	3B 42
Manor Fell WA7: Pal F	2H 51
Manor Ind. Est. WA4: Westy	2G 33
Manor Lock WA4: Warr	1G 33
MANOR PARK	3A 42
Manor Pk. WA7: Mnr P	3A 42
Manor Park Bus. Pk.	
WA7: Mnr P	3H 41
Manor Pk. Ct. WA7: Mnr P	3A 42
Manor Pl. WA8: Wid	4D 26
Manor Rd. WA6: Frod	2C 56
WA7: Run	5D 40
WA8: Wid	4B 28
WA13: Lymm	3C 36
(not continuous)	
Manorwood Dr. L35: Whis	1A 14
Manse Field Rd. WA6: K'ley	6G 57
Mansell Cl. WA8: Wid	6B 16
Mansfield Cl. WA3: Bchwd	5G 11
Manston Rd. WA5: Penk	2D 30
Manuel Perez Rd.	
WA5: Gt San	5F 19
Manx Rd. WA4: Warr	2D 32
Maple Av. WA3: Low	1A 4
WA7: Run	1C 50
WA7: Sut W	5G 51
WA8: Wid	4B 28
Maple Cres. WA5: Penk	1D 30
Maple Gro. WA4: Warr	2F 33
Maple Rd. M31: Part	6H 13
WA1: W'ston	4E 23
WA2: Win	3D 8
Mapleton Dr. WA7: Sut W	6F 51
Maplewood Cl. WA8: Wid	6C 26
Mapplewell Cres.	
WA5: Gt San	5E 19
Marbury St. WA4: Warr	2E 33
Marcien Way WA8: Wid	2H 27
Marcross Cl. WA5: Call	2A 20
Mardale Av. WA2: Warr	6D 8
Mardale Cres. WA13: Lymm	1D 36
Margaret Av. WA1: W'ston	4B 22
Margaret Ct. WA8: Wid	6B 28
Marian Cl. L35: R'hill	1E 15
Marian Dr. L35: R'hill	1D 14
Marie Dr. WA4: Thel	3D 34
Marina Av. WA5: Gt San	1F 31
Marina Dr. WA2: Warr	2E 21
Marina Gro. WA7: Run	5B 40
Marina La. WA7: Murd	2C 52
Marina Village WA7: Pres B	2C 52
Marine Av. M31: Part	6H 13
Mariner Cl. WA7: Murd	3B 52
Marion Dr. WA7: West	3H 49
Market Ga. WA1: Warr	6D 20

Netherfield—Pasture La.

Netherfield WA8: Wid .5F 27
Netherley Rd. L35: Tar G .2A 26
WA8: Wid .2A 26
NETHERTON .4A 56
Netherton Dr. WA6: Frod .4A 56
Nevada Cl. WA5: Gt San .3G 19
Neville Av. WA2: Warr .2F 21
Neville Cres. WA5: Penk .2E 31
New Albert Ter. *WA7: Run .4B 40*
(off Bold St.)
New Bank Pl. WA8: Wid .4D 26
New Bank Rd. WA8: Wid .4D 26
New Barnet WA8: Wid .1H 27
Newborough Cl. WA5: Call .1H 19
New Bri. WA1: Warr .1D 32
Newbridge Cl. WA5: Call .1G 19
WA7: Brook .3A 52
Newburgh Cl. WA7: Wind H .6B 42
Newbury Cl. WA8: Wid .1A 28
Newchurch La. WA3: Cul .5F 5
Newcombe Av. WA2: P'gate .3G 21
New Cut Ind. Est.
WA1: W'ston .4C 22
New Cut La. WA1: W'ston .4B 22
Newfield Ct. WA13: Lymm .6E 25
Newfield Rd. WA13: Lymm .2B 36
Newfield Ter. WA6: Hel .3D 60
New Hall La. WA3: Ris .6E 5
(not continuous)
New Hampshire Cl.
WA5: Gt San .4F 19
Newhaven Rd. WA2: Warr .5D 8
Newington Way WA8: Wid .2H 27
Newland Cl. WA8: Wid .2E 27
Newland M. WA3: Cul .2E 5
Newlands Cl. WA6: Frod .5C 56
Newlands Rd. WA4: S Hth .3H 33
New La. WA3: Croft .2A 10
WA4: App T .2B 46
NEW LANE END .5A 4
New La. End WA3: Croft .5A 4
Newlyn Cl. WA7: Brook .3H 51
Newlyn Gdns. WA5: Penk .2B 30
New Mnr. Rd. WA4: Pres H .3E 53
Newman St. WA4: Westy .1H 33
New Mkt. Hall *WA7: Run .4A 40*
(off Church St.)
New Market Wlk. WA1: Warr .6D 20
Newmoore La. WA7: Nort .4C 42
New Moss Rd. M44: Cad .3H 13
Newquay Cl. WA7: Brook .3A 52
New Rd. WA4: Warr .1E 33
(not continuous)
WA13: Lymm .2C 36
Newsham Cl. WA8: Wid .1D 26
Newsholme Cl. WA3: Cul .4F 5
Newstead Rd. WA8: Wid .1B 38
New St. WA4: Warr .1E 33
WA7: Run .5A 40
WA8: Wid .5B 28
Newton Av. WA3: Ris .4E 11
Newton Bank WA4: Dares .1F 53
Newton Gro. WA2: Fearn .6H 9
Newton La. WA4: Dares .1F 53
WA4: Dares, Lwr Wh .2H 53
Newton Rd. WA2: Win .1B 8
NEWTOWN .2D 56
Nicholas Rd. WA8: Wid .5E 27
Nicholls St. WA4: Grap .3B 34
Nicholson St. WA1: Warr .6B 20
Nickleford Hall Dr.
WA8: Wid .5H 15
Nicol Av. WA3: W'ston .3F 23
Nigel Wlk. WA7: Cas .5G 41
Nightingale Cl.
WA3: Bchwd .5F 11
WA7: Beech .4F 51
Noble Cl. WA3: Bchwd .6E 11
Nook La. WA2: Fearn .1B 22
WA4: Westy .2A 34
Nora St. WA1: Warr .6E 21
Norbreck Cl. WA5: Gt San .2E 31
Norbury Av. WA2: Warr .3F 21
Norbury Cl. WA8: Wid .4D 28
Norbury Fold L35: R'hill .2G 15
Norcott Av. WA4: S Hth .3F 33
Norcott Dr. WA5: B'wood .3D 6
Norden Cl. WA3: Bchwd .4C 10
Norfolk Cl. M44: Cad .4G 13
Norfolk Dr. WA5: Gt San .5C 18
Norfolk Pl. WA8: Wid .5E 27
Norfolk St. WA7: Run .4B 40
Norgrove Cl. WA7: Murd .1B 52
Norland's La. L35: R'hill .3G 15
WA8: Cron .3G 15
WA8: Wid .5H 15
Norlands Pk. WA8: Wid .5H 15
Norland St. WA8: Wid .4D 28
Norleane Cres. WA7: Run .1B 50
Norley Cl. WA5: Warr .5A 20
Normanby Cl. WA5: Warr .4A 20
Norman Rd. WA7: Run .6A 40
Norman St. WA2: Warr .5D 20
Norreys Av. WA5: Warr .3B 20
Norris St. WA2: Warr .3E 21
North Av. WA2: Warr .3D 20
NORTH CHESHIRE BUPA HOSPITAL
.6F 45
Northdale Rd. WA1: P'ton .3A 22
Northern La. WA8: Wid .2C 26
North Front L35: Whis .2A 14
Northolt Ct. WA2: P'gate .2G 21
North Pk. Brook Rd.
WA5: Call .1A 20
North Vw. WA5: Gt San .4C 18
Northway WA2: Warr .2D 20
WA7: Pal F .1F 51
WA8: Wid .4F 27
WA13: Lymm .1B 36
North West Face
(Indoor Climbing Wall) .4C 20
Northwich Rd. WA4: Dutt .5D 52
WA4: Lwr S .6G 45
WA7: Brook .4H 51
WA7: Dutt, Pres B .5B 52
Northwood Rd. WA7: Run .5E 41
NORTON .1B 52
Norton Av. WA5: Penk .6C 18
Norton Ga. WA7: Nort .1A 52
Norton Hill WA7: Wind H .6A 42
Norton La. WA7: Halt, Nort .1G 51
(not continuous)
WA7: Nort .6B 42
Norton Priory .4H 41
Norton Priory Gdns. .4H 41
Norton Sta. Rd.
WA7: Murd, Nort .1B 52
Norton Vw. WA7: Halt .1G 51
Norton Village WA7: Nort .1B 52
Nortonwood La.
WA7: Wind H .1A 52
Nottingham Cl. WA1: W'ston .5E 23
Nursery Cl. WA8: Wid .2D 28
Nursery Rd. WA1: P'gate .3H 21
Nuttall Ct. WA3: Bchwd .5C 10

O

Oak Av. M44: Cad .4H 13
Oakdale Av. WA4: S Hth .4F 33
WA6: Frod .5D 56
Oakdene Av. WA1: W'ston .4C 22
Oakdene Ct. L35: R'hill .1E 15
Oak Dr. WA7: Run .2C 50
Oakfield Dr. WA8: Wid .5C 26
Oaklands L35: R'hill .1E 15
Oaklands Dr. WA13: Lymm .3B 36
Oakland St. WA1: Warr .4G 21
WA8: Wid .3A 40
Oak Mdws. L35: R'hill .2G 15
Oakmere Dr. WA5: Penk .2D 30
Oakmere St. WA7: Run .5A 40
Oak Rd. M31: Part .1H 25
WA5: Penk .2D 30
WA13: Lymm .2A 36
Oaks Cl. WA9: Clock F .1D 16
Oaks Pl. WA8: Wid .6A 28
Oakston Av. L35: R'hill .1F 15
Oak St. WA3: Croft .2A 10
Oakways WA4: App .2F 45
Oak Wharf M. WA4: App .5E 33
OAKWOOD .6F 11
Oakwood Av. WA1: Warr .4F 21
Oakwood Ga. WA3: Bchwd .5D 10
Oakwood Mt. WA3: Bchwd .6F 11
Oban Gro. WA2: Fearn .6A 10
Oil Sites Rd. CH65: Ell P .1B 58
Okell St. WA7: Run .5A 40
Old Albert Ter. *WA7: Run .4B 40*
(off Thomas St.)
Old Cherry La. WA13: Lymm .1G 47
Old Chester Rd. WA4: Dares .6F 43
WA4: H Walt .6B 32
WA6: Hel .2D 60
Old Coach Rd. WA7: Run .4H 39
Old Cryers La. CH2: Elt .3E 59
Oldfield Rd. WA13: Lymm .1H 35
(not continuous)
Oldgate WA8: Wid .6E 27
OLD HALL .3G 19
Old Hall Cl. WA4: H Walt .5C 32
Old Hall La. CH2: Elt .3E 59
Old Hall Rd. WA5: Old H .3H 19
Oldham St. WA4: Warr .2F 33
Old Hey Wlk. WA12: New W .1G 7
Old Higher Rd.
WA8: Hale B .2A 38
Old La. L35: R'hill .1D 14
Old Liverpool Rd.
WA5: Warr .1H 31
Old Market Pl. *WA1: Warr .6D 20*
(off Horsemarket St.)
Old Mill Cl. WA13: Lymm .5G 25
Old Orchard L35: Whis .2A 14
Old Pewterspear La.
WA4: App .4F 45
Old Quay St. WA7: Run .4B 40
Old Rd. WA4: Warr .1D 32
Old School Ho. La.
WA2: Win .2C 8
Old Smithy La.
WA13: Lymm .3A 36
Old Upton La. WA8: Wid .1G 27
O'Leary St. WA2: Warr .4E 21
Oliver St. WA2: Warr .5D 20
Ollerton Cl. WA4: Grap .2B 34
Ollerton Pk. WA5: B'wood .2C 6
Ollier St. WA8: Wid .6A 28
Omega Blvd. WA5: Gt San .2B 18
Openshaw La. M44: Cad .3H 13
Orange Gro. WA2: Warr .1G 21
Orchard, The WA6: Hel .3D 60
Orchard Av. WA13: Lymm .2D 36
Orchard Brow WA3: Rix .1E 25
Orchard Cl. L35: Whis .2A 14
WA6: Frod .5A 56
Orchard Ct. WA3: Croft .1A 10
WA6: Frod .3A 56
Orchard Gdns. L35: Whis .3A 14
Orchard Pk. Cvn. Pk.
CH2: Elt .1F 59
Orchard Pk. La. CH2: Elt .1F 59
Orchard Pl. WA6: Hel .1E 61
Orchard Rd. WA13: Lymm .6F 25
Orchard St. WA1: Warr .6E 21
WA2: Fearn .1A 22
WA4: S Hth .5E 33
Orchard Wlk. *WA7: Pal F .2F 51*
(off Halton Lea Shop. Cen.)
Orchard Way WA8: Wid .2C 26
Ordnance Av. WA3: Bchwd .6E 11
ORFORD .1F 21
Orford Av. WA2: Warr .4E 21
Orford Cl. L24: Hale .5A 38
Orford Grn. WA2: Warr .2F 21
Orford La. WA2: Warr .5D 20
Orford Rd. WA1: Warr .3F 21
WA2: Warr .3F 21
Orford St. WA1: Warr .6D 20
Orion Blvd. WA5: Gt San .2C 18
Orkney Cl. WA8: Wid .2E 29
Ormond Cl. WA8: Wid .3E 27
Orrell Cl. WA5: Gt San .5E 19
Osborne Av. WA2: Warr .2F 21
Osborne Rd. WA4: Walt .4D 32
Osier Cl. CH2: Elt .2G 59
Osprey Cl. WA2: Warr .6G 9
WA7: Beech .4F 51
Ossett Cl. WA7: Nort .1B 52
OUGHTRINGTON .1F 37
Oughtrington Cres.
WA13: Lymm .1F 37
Oughtrington La.
WA13: Lymm .3E 37
Oughtrington Vw.
WA13: Lymm .1F 37
Oulton Ct. WA4: Grap .3B 34
OVERTON .4C 56
Overton Dr. WA6: Frod .5C 56
Ovington Cl. WA7: Sut W .5F 51
Owen Rd. L35: R'hill .1E 15
Owens Corner Rdbt.
WA4: App .4F 45
Owen St. WA2: Warr .4C 20
Oxborough Cl. WA8: Wid .2H 27
Oxenham Rd. WA2: Warr .6C 8
Oxford Gro. M44: Cad .3G 13
Oxford Rd. WA7: Run .6A 40
Oxford St. WA4: Warr .1E
WA8: Wid .6B
Oxheys WA7: Nort .1A
Oxmead Cl. WA2: P'gate .2B
Oxmoor Cl. WA7: Brook .4G
Oxton Cl. WA8: Wid .1E

P

PADDINGTON .3H
Paddington Bank WA1: Warr .5H
Paddock, The CH2: Elt .2E
WA6: Hel .3E
WA13: Lymm .2G
Paddock La. WA13: Warb .3F
Paddock Ri. WA7: Beech .5E
Padgate Bus. Cen.
WA1: P'gate .3B
(off Green L...
Padgate La. WA1: Warr .4F
(not continuou...
Padgate Recreation Cen. .1H
Padgate Station (Rail) .2A
Padstow Cl. WA5: Penk .2C
Padstow Sq. WA7: Brook .4H
Page La. WA8: Wid .4C
Paignton Cl. WA5: Penk .1C
PALACE FIELDS .3G
Palacefields Av. WA7: Pal F .3F
Palatine Ind. Est. WA4: Warr .2E
Palin Dr. WA5: Gt San .5D
Palliser Cl. WA3: Bchwd .6G
Palmer Cres. WA5: Old H .3H
Palmwood Av. L35: R'hill .1F
Palmyra Ho. WA1: Warr .6C
Palmyra Sq. Nth. WA1: Warr .6C
Palmyra Sq. Sth. WA1: Warr .6C
Pangbourne Cl. WA4: App .1G
Paragon Cl. WA8: Wid .6B
Parbold Ct. WA8: Wid .5F
Park, The WA5: Penk .2B
(not continuou...
Park Av. WA4: Warr .2F
WA8: Wid .3B
Park Blvd. WA1: Warr .1C
Park Ct. WA1: Warr .6B
WA6: Frod .3A
WA7: Run .1A
Park Cres. WA4: App .1F
Parkdale Ind. Est. WA1: Warr .1E
Parkdale Rd. WA1: P'ton .4A
Parkers Ct. WA7: Pal F .3E
Parker St. WA1: Warr .1C
WA7: Run .4B
Parkfield Av. WA4: Westy .1A
Parkfield Dr. WA6: Hel .2D
Parkfields La. WA2: Fearn .1H
Parkgate Rd. WA4: S Hth .4F
Parkgate Way WA7: Murd .3A
Parkland Cl. WA4: App T .2B
Parklands WA8: Wid .2E
Parklands Dr. CH2: Elt .2E
Park La. WA4: App, H Walt .2A
WA6: Frod .3B
WA13: Warb .2G
Park Pl. WA1: Warr .6C
Park Rd. CH2: Thor M .4C
WA2: Warr .2F
WA5: Gt San .4A
WA7: Run .1H
WA8: Wid .4B
WA13: Lymm .5H
WA13: Warb .3F
(not continuous)
Parkside Ct. WA8: Wid .3A
Parksway WA1: W'ston .4D
Park Vw. WA2: Warr .6G
Parkview Pk. WA13: Lymm .4H
Parkwood Cl. WA13: Lymm .3B
Parkwood Rd. L35: Whis .1A
Parlington Cl. WA8: Wid .6E
Parr St. WA1: Warr .1E
(not continuous)
WA8: Wid .4C
Parrs Wood Vw. WA4: Grap .4A
Parry Dr. WA4: Thel .2E
Parry's La. WA7: Run .6A
Parsonage Rd. WA8: Wid .3A
Parsonage Way WA5: Gt San .5E
Partridge Cl. WA3: Bchwd .5E
Pasture Dr. WA3: Croft .2A
Pasture La. WA2: P'gate .2B

74 A-Z Warrington

Redtail Cl.—Sankey Grn.

Redtail Cl. WA7: Run 4H 39
Redvales Ct. WA3: Bchwd 5C 10
Redwood Cl. WA1: W'ston 5E 23
Redwood Dr. CH2: Elt 1G 59
Reedgate La. CW9: Ant 6E 47
Reedsmere Cl. WA4: S Hth 3G 33
Refuge Sq. WA5: Warr 4C 20
Regal Cres. WA8: Wid 5D 26
Regency Pk. WA8: Wid 2G 27
Regency Sq. WA5: Warr 4B 20
Regent Av. WA1: P'gate 3A 22
Regent Rd. WA8: Wid 4B 28
Regent St. WA1: Warr 6C 20
WA7: Run 4A 40
Reid Av. WA5: Warr 3B 20
Rembury Pl. WA4: Dutt 6D 52
Rendlesham Cl.
WA3: Bchwd 3H 11
Renown Cl. WA3: Ris 5D 10
Renton Av. WA7: Run 5D 40
Revesby Cl. WA8: Wid 3F 27
Reynolds Av. WA3: Ris 4E 11
Reynolds St. WA4: Westy 2G 33
Rhodes St. WA2: Warr 4E 21
Rhona Dr. WA5: Gt San 5C 18
Rhyl St. WA8: Wid 6H 27
Ribble Av. L35: R'hill 1E 15
Ribble Cl. WA3: Cul 5F 5
WA8: Wid 2F 29
Ribchester Gdns. WA3: Cul 4G 5
Richard Cl. WA7: Cas 6G 41
Richardson St. WA2: Warr 3E 21
Richmond Av. WA4: Grap 2C 34
WA4: Westy 1H 33
WA7: Run 5E 41
Richmond Cl. WA3: Cul 3D 4
WA13: Lymm 1F 37
Richmond Dr. WA13: Lymm 1F 37
Richmond St. WA4: Westy 2A 34
WA8: Wid 4C 28
Ridding La. WA7: Brook 4H 51
Ridgebourne Cl. WA5: Call 1H 19
Ridgeway, The WA6: Frod 2H 61
WA7: Murd 3B 52
WA8: Cron 5E 15
Ridgeway (Country Holiday Pk.), The
WA6: Frod 3H 61
Ridgway Gdns. WA13: Lymm 2B 36
Ridgway St. WA2: Warr 4F 21
Ridley Dr. WA5: Gt San 1G 31
Ridsdale WA8: Wid 5E 27
Riley Dr. WA7: Run 1A 50
Rilston Av. WA3: Cul 4D 4
Rimington Cl. WA3: Cul 4E 5
Ringway Rd. WA7: Run 5D 40
Ringwood Cl. WA3: Bchwd 4H 11
Ripley St. WA5: Warr 4A 20
Ripon Row WA7: Run 2D 50
RISLEY 3E 11
Risley Employment Area
WA3: Ris 2F 11
Risley Moss Local Nature Reserve
.....5H 11
Risley Moss Local Nature Reserve
Vis. Cen. 4G 11
Risley Rd. WA3: Ris 4F 11
River Rd. WA4: Warr 2D 32
(not continuous)
Riversdale WA1: W'ston 4F 23
WA6: Frod 2C 56
Riversdale Rd. WA7: Halt 6E 41
Riverside Cl. WA1: Warr 1E 33
Riverside Retail Pk.
WA1: Warr 1E 33
Riverside Trad. Est.
WA5: Cuerd 4B 30
River Vw. Residential Cvn. Pk.
WA8: Wid 5C 28
River Wlk. *WA7: Pal F* *2F 51*
(off Halton Lea Shop. Cen.)
Rivington Ct. WA1: W'ston 3E 23
Rivington Gro. M44: Cad 3H 13
Rivington Rd. WA7: Pres B 6C 52
RIXTON 1D 24
Rixton Av. WA5: Warr 3B 20
Rixton Claypits Nature Reserve
.....1C 24
Rixton Pk. Homes WA3: Rix 1D 24
Roberts Ct. WA7: Pal F 3F 51
Roberts Fold WA3: Bchwd 5D 10
Robert St. WA5: Warr 5B 20
WA7: Run 5C 40
WA8: Wid 4B 28
Robin Cl. WA7: Murd 2B 52
Robin Hood La. WA6: Hel 4D 60
Robins La. WA3: Cul 5D 4
Robson St. WA1: Warr 5F 21
Roby Gro. WA5: Gt San 5E 19
Rochester Cl. WA5: Gt San 6G 19
Rock, The WA6: Hel 3D 60
Rock Dr. WA6: Frod 2C 56
Rockfield Cl. WA8: Wid 3F 27
Rockfield Dr. WA6: Hel 3E 61
Rockingham Cl. WA3: Bchwd 3H 11
Rock La. WA8: Wid 1H 27
Rock Rd. WA4: Westy 1G 33
Rocksavage Way WA7: Run 4A 50
Roddy La. WA6: K'ley 5H 57
Rodgers Cl. WA6: Frod 2B 56
Roeburn Way WA5: Penk 2B 30
Roehampton Dr. WA7: Pal F 2E 51
Roemarsh Ct. WA7: Pal F 3E 51
Rokeby Ct. WA7: Mnr P 2B 42
Roland Av. WA7: Run 6H 39
Rolands Wlk. WA7: Cas 5F 41
Rolleston St. WA2: Warr 5C 20
Roman Cl. WA7: Cas 5E 41
Roman Rd. WA4: S Hth 4E 33
Romney Cl. WA8: Wid 3E 29
Ronald Dr. WA2: Fearn 1B 22
Ronaldshay WA8: Wid 3E 29
Ronan Rd. WA8: Wid 2F 39
Roome St. WA2: Warr 4E 21
Roper's Bri. Cl. L35: Whis 1A 14
Rosam Ct. WA7: Pal F 3E 51
Roscoe Av. WA2: Warr 3F 21
Roscoe Cres. WA7: West P 2G 49
Roscommon Way WA8: Wid 2G 27
Rose Bank WA13: Lymm 2C 36
Rosebank Rd. M44: Cad 6G 13
Rose Cl. WA7: Murd 4B 52
Rose Cres. WA8: Wid 6H 27
Rosedale Av. WA1: W'ston 4C 22
Rose Lea Cl. WA8: Wid 1A 28
Rosemary Av. WA4: S Hth 3G 33
WA7: Beech 5F 51
Rosemary Cl. WA5: Gt San 5G 19
Rosemoor Gdns. WA4: App 2H 45
Rose Mt. WA2: Win 1D 8
Rose St. WA8: Wid 6H 27
Rose Vw. Av. WA8: Wid 3A 28
Rosewood Av. WA1: Warr 4G 21
WA6: Frod 4D 56
Rosewood Cl. WA8: Wid 5D 26
Rosewood Farm Ct.
WA8: Wid 6G 15
Rossall Cl. L24: Hale 5A 38
Rossall Rd. WA5: Gt San 1F 31
WA8: Wid 3D 28
Ross Cl. WA5: Old H 3H 19
Rossendale Dr. WA3: Bchwd 3G 11
Rossett Cl. WA5: Call 1A 20
Ross St. WA8: Wid 4B 28
Rostherne Cl. WA5: Warr 1H 31
Rostherne Cres. WA8: Wid 3F 27
Rosyth Cl. WA2: Fearn 6H 9
Rothay Dr. WA5: Penk 2B 30
Rothbury Cl. WA7: Beech 3E 51
Rothbury Ct. WA9: Sut M 1B 16
Rothesay Cl. WA7: Cas 5F 41
Roughlea Av. WA3: Cul 3D 4
Roughley Av. WA5: Warr 1H 31
Roundabout, The
WA8: Cron 5F 15
Round Thorn WA3: Croft 2A 10
Routledge St. WA8: Wid 4B 28
Rowan Av. WA3: Low 1A 4
Rowan Cl. WA5: Gt San 5D 18
WA7: Run 2C 50
Rowland Cl. WA2: Fearn 6A 10
ROWLINSON'S GREEN 2H 47
Rowson Dr. M44: Cad 3H 13
Rowthorn Cl. WA8: Wid 5G 27
Roxborough Cl.
WA5: B'wood 3E 7
Royal Av. WA8: Wid 4D 26
Royal London Bus. Pk.
WA5: W'brk 6A 8
Royal Pl. WA8: Wid 5D 26
Royden Av. WA7: Run 1H 49
Royleen Dr. WA6: Frod 5D 56
Royston Av. WA1: P'ton 4H 21
Rozel Cres. WA5: Gt San 1F 31
Rudgate L35: Whis 1A 14
Rudheath La. WA7: Nort 4B 42
Rudloe Ct. WA2: P'gate 2G 21
Rufford Cl. WA8: Wid 3E 27
Rufford Ct. WA1: W'ston 3E 23
Ruislip Ct. WA2: P'gate 2H 21
RUNCORN 4A 40
Runcorn Dock Rd.
WA7: Run 5G 39
Runcorn East Station (Rail) 2B 52
Runcorn Hill Local Nature Reserve
.....1H 49
Runcorn Hill Local Nature Reserve
Vis. Cen. 1H 49
Runcorn Rd.
WA4: Dares, H Walt, Moore
.....3D 42
Runcorn Ski & Snowboard Cen.
.....2H 51
Runcorn Spur Rd. WA7: Run 5B 40
Runcorn Station (Rail) 5H 39
Runcorn Swimming Pool *4B 40*
(off Bridge St.)
Runnymead Wlk. *WA8: Wid* *3C 28*
(off William St.)
Runnymede WA1: W'ston 4D 22
Runnymede Ct. *WA8: Wid* *4C 28*
(off William St.)
Runnymede Gdns. *WA8: Wid* *4C 28*
(off Cliffe St.)
Rupert Row WA7: Cas 1G 51
Ruscolm Cl. WA5: Gt San 4B 18
Rushes Mdw. WA13: Lymm 6F 25
Rushfield Cres. WA7: Brook 4H 51
Rush Gdns. WA13: Lymm 1E 37
RUSHGREEN 1E 37
Rushgreen Rd. WA13: Lymm 1D 36
Rushmore Dr. WA8: Wid 2H 27
Rushmore Gro. WA1: P'ton 4A 22
Rushton Cl. WA5: B'wood 2D 6
WA8: Wid 2H 27
Ruskin Av. WA2: Warr 1E 21
Russell Ct. WA8: Wid 1B 28
Russell Rd. WA7: Run 6G 39
Ruthin Cl. WA5: Call 6A 8
Ruthin Wlk. WA6: Hel 4C 60
Rutland Av. WA4: Walt 5D 32
Rutland Rd. M31: Part 1H 25
M44: Cad 4H 13
Rutland St. WA7: Run 4H 39
Rutter Av. WA5: Warr 1B 20
Rydal Av. WA4: Warr 3C 32
Rydal Gro. WA6: Hel 4D 60
WA7: Run 1B 50
Rydal Way WA8: Wid 4E 27
Ryder Rd. WA1: W'ston 3C 22
WA8: Wid 1B 28
Ryecroft CH2: Elt 2F 59
Ryfields Village WA2: Warr 3F 21
Rylands St. WA1: Warr 6D 20
WA8: Wid 5B 28

S

Sabre Cl. WA7: Murd 2B 52
Saddlers Ri. WA7: Nort 1A 52
Sadler St. WA8: Wid 4C 28
Saffron Cl. WA2: P'gate 2B 22
Sage Cl. WA2: P'gate 1C 22
St Alban Rd. WA5: Penk 6C 18
St Ambrose Rd. WA8: Wid 4C 28
St Andrews Cl. WA2: Fearn 5A 10
St Andrews Ho. WA3: Ris 3D 10
St Anne's Av. WA4: Grap 3B 34
St Anne's Av. E. WA4: Grap 3B 34
St Annes Rd. WA8: Wid 3B 28
St Anthony Pl. WA2: Win 3D 8
St Asaph Dr. WA5: Call 6H 7
St Augustine's Av.
WA4: Westy 1H 33
St Austell Cl. WA5: Penk 2C 30
WA7: Brook 3H 51
St Austins La. WA1: Warr 1D 32
St Barnabas Pl. WA5: Warr 5A 20
St Benedict's Cl. WA2: Warr 4D 20
St Benedict's Pl. WA2: Warr 4D 20
St Brides Cl. WA5: Penk 2C 30
St Bridget's Cl. WA2: Fearn 6H 9
St David's Dr. WA5: Call 1A 20
St Elphins Cl. WA1: Warr 6E 21
St Georges Cl. WA4: App 4G 45
St Georges Ct. WA8: Wid 5F 27
St Helens Cl. WA3: Rix 6F 13
St Helens Linkway
L35: R'hill 1H 15
St Hilda's Dr. WA6: Frod 2
St James Cl. WA6: Frod 2
St James' Ct. WA4: Warr 1
St James Mt. L35: R'hill 1
St James Rd. L35: R'hill 1
St John Av. WA4: Warr 3
St Johns Brow WA7: Run 4
St John's Ct. WA1: Warr 4
St John St. WA7: Run 4
St Johns Vs. WA8: Wid 3
St Joseph's Cl. WA5: Penk 6
St Katherines Way
WA1: Warr 6
St Lawrence Rd. WA6: Frod 4
St Luke's Cres. WA8: Wid 1
St Luke's Way WA6: Frod 2E
St Margaret's Av. WA2: Warr 2
St Martin's La. WA7: Murd 2E
St Mary's Cl. L24: Hale 5A
WA4: App 1E
St Mary's Grn. WA1: Warr 6E
St Marys Rd. WA7: Halt 6F
WA8: Wid 3A
WA5: Gt San, Penk 6D
St Mary's St. WA4: Warr 1E
St Matthews Cl. WA4: App 6F
St Mawes Cl. WA8: Wid 3G
St Mawgan Ct. WA2: P'gate 1H
St Michael's Cl. WA8: Wid 6E
St Michael's Ind. Est.
WA8: Wid 6E
St Michael's Rd. WA8: Wid 6E
St Monica's Cl. WA4: App 6G
St Oswalds Cl. WA2: Win 3
St Paul's Rd. WA8: Wid 6A
St Peter's Cl. WA13: Lymm 1E
St Peters Ct. WA2: Warr 5E
St Peter's Way WA2: Warr 5D
ST ROCCO'S HOSPICE 4A
St Stephen Rd.
WA5: Gt San, Penk 6D
St Stephen's Av. WA2: Warr 6D
St Thomas Ct. WA8: Wid 4F
St Vincent Rd. WA5: Penk 6D
St Wilfrid's Dr. WA4: Grap 4C
Salisbury St. WA1: Warr 5F
WA7: Run 6A
WA8: Wid 5B
Saltash Cl. WA7: Brook 3H 5
Salton Gdns. WA5: Warr 4A
Saltwood Dr. WA7: Brook 4A 5
Saltworks Cl. WA6: Frod 1D 5
Samuel St. WA5: Warr 1A
Sanbec Gdns. WA8: Cron 6F 1
Sandalwood WA7: Nort 6A 4
Sandalwood Cl. WA2: Warr 1F
Sanders Hey Cl. WA7: Brook 4G 5
Sanderson Cl. WA5: Gt San 5B 1
Sandfield Ct. WA6: Frod 3B 5
Sandfield Cres. WA3: G'bury 6H
Sandfields WA6: Frod 3B 5
Sandhill Ter. WA4: Latch 2G 3
Sandhurst St. WA4: Westy 2H 3
Sandicroft Cl. WA3: Bchwd 4C 1
Sandiway Av. WA8: Wid 4C 2
Sandon Pl. WA8: Wid 4D 2
Sandown Cl. WA3: Cul 3F 5
WA7: Run 3B 50
Sandringham Av. WA6: Hel 2D 60
Sandringham Dr.
WA5: Gt San 1G 31
Sandringham Rd. WA8: Wid 1H 27
Sandstone Cl. L35: R'hill 2E 15
Sandstone M. WA8: Wid 1G 27
Sandy La. WA2: Warr 6D 8
WA3: Croft 1A 10
WA4: S Hth 5F 33
WA5: Penk 1E 31
WA6: Hel 3D 60
WA7: Pres B 3C 52
WA7: West P 2F 49
WA8: Cron 6F 15
WA8: Wid 5G 17
WA13: Lymm 6F 25
Sandy La. W. WA2: Warr 6C 8
Sandy Moor La. WA7: Nort 5B 42
Sandymoor La. WA7: Nort 4B 42
SANKEY BRIDGES 1H 31
Sankey Bridges Ind. Est.
WA5: Gt San 1G 31
Sankey (for Penketh) Station (Rail)
.....5D 18
Sankey Grn. WA5: Warr 6A 20

76 A-Z Warrington

Sankey Mnr.—Stringer Cres.

Sankey Mnr. WA5: Gt San 5D 18
Sankey St. WA1: Warr 6C 20
(not continuous)
WA8: Wid 1A 40
Sankey Valley Country Pk.
WA12: New W 1G 7
Sankey Way WA5: Gt San 6E 19
WA5: Warr 6B 20
Sanky La. WA4: Hatt 6B 44
Sarus Ct. WA7: Mnr P 3H 41
Saundersfoot Cl.
WA5: Call 1A 20
Saville Av. WA5: Warr 4B 20
Sawley Cl. WA3: Cul 5G 5
WA7: Murd 2C 52
Saxon Cl. WA4: App 2D 44
Saxon Rd. WA7: Run 5C 40
Saxon Ter. WA8: Wid 4B 28
Sayce St. WA8: Wid 4B 28
Scafell Av. WA2: Warr 6E 9
Scholars Grn. La.
WA13: Lymm 2D 36
School Brow WA1: Warr 6E 21
School La. CH2: Elt 2E 59
L35: R'hill 2G 15
(not continuous)
M44: Cad 4H 13
WA3: Ris 4A 12
WA3: Rix 1E 25
WA6: Frod 4C 56
WA7: Halt 1F 51
WA8: Bold H 4E 17
School Rd. WA2: Warr 2E 21
School St. WA4: Warr 1D 32
School Way WA8: Wid 2D 28
Schooner Cl. WA7: Murd 3B 52
Science Pk. Nth. WA3: Ris 3D 10
Science Pk. Sth. WA3: Ris 4D 10
Scotland Rd. WA1: Warr 6D 20
Scott Av. WA8: Wid 5H 27
WA9: Sut M 1A 16
Scott St. WA2: Warr 5D 20
Seabury St. WA4: Westy 2A 34
Seaford Cl. WA7: Wind H 6B 42
Seaford Pl. WA2: Warr 5C 8
Sealand Cl. WA2: P'gate 3G 21
Sea La. WA7: Run 5D 40
Seathwaite Cl. WA7: Beech 4E 51
Seaton Pk. WA7: Nort 4C 42
Seattle Cl. WA5: Gt San 4F 19
Secker Av. WA4: Latch 3F 33
Secker Cres. WA4: Latch 3F 33
Second Av. WA7: Pal F 1F 51
Sedbergh Gro. WA7: Beech 4E 51
Sedgewick Cres.
WA5: B'wood 3C 6
Sefton Av. WA8: Wid 2A 28
Selborne L35: Whis 1B 14
Selby Cl. WA7: Nort 3D 42
Selby St. WA5: Warr 6A 20
(not continuous)
Selkirk Av. WA4: Westy 2A 34
Selworthy Dr. WA4: Thel 2D 34
Selwyn Cl. WA8: Wid 2D 28
Seneschal Ct. WA7: Pal F 3E 51
Sennen Cl. WA7: Brook 4H 51
Sephton Av. WA3: Cul 4E 5
Sergeant York Loop
WA5: Gt San 5F 19
Severn Cl. WA2: Warr 1G 21
WA8: Wid 3E 29
Severn Rd. L35: R'hill 1D 14
WA3: Cul 5F 5
Sewell St. WA7: Run 5B 40
Sextant Cl. WA7: Murd 4B 52
Seymour Ct. WA7: Mnr P 3A 42
Seymour Dr.
WA1: P'ton, P'gate 4A 22
Shackleton Cl. WA5: Old H 3G 19
Shadewood Cres. WA4: Grap . . .3B 34
Shaftesbury Av. WA5: Penk 3C 30
Shaftesbury Way
WA5: B'wood 2D 6
Shakespeare Gro.
WA2: Warr 1E 21
(not continuous)
Shakespeare Rd. WA8: Wid 4A 28
WA9: Sut M 1A 16
Shanklin Cl. WA5: Gt San 5A 18
Shannon Gro. WA8: Wid 3G 27
Sharon Pk. Cl. WA4: Grap 4C 34
Sharp St. WA2: Warr 4D 20
WA8: Wid 5A 28
Shawbury Gro. WA1: P'gate 3A 22
Shawell Ct. WA8: Wid 3E 29
Shaw Entry L35: Whis 3B 14
Shaw's Av. WA2: Warr 3D 20
Shaw St. WA3: Cul 4G 5
WA7: Run 5H 39
(not continuous)
Sheerwater Cl. WA1: P'gate 3H 21
Sheffield Cl. WA5: Gt San 6G 19
Sheffield Row WA12: New W 1H 7
Shelagh Av. WA8: Wid 4A 28
Shelley Gro. WA4: Westy 1H 33
Shelley Rd. WA8: Wid 4A 28
Shelley St. WA9: Sut M 1B 16
SHELL GREEN 4D 28
Shell Green Est., The
WA8: Wid 5E 29
Shell Grn. Ho. WA8: Wid 5E 29
Shelton Cl. WA8: Wid 2E 29
Shepcroft La. WA4: S'ton 5E 45
Shepherds Row WA7: Cas 5F 41
Shepperton Cl. WA4: App 1G 45
Sherborne Cl. WA7: Nort 4D 42
Sherbourne Way
WA5: B'wood 3D 6
Sheridan Pl. WA2: Win 4C 8
Sheridan Way WA7: Nort 5B 42
Sheringham Rd.
WA5: Gt San 5C 18
Sherman Dr. L35: R'hill 2F 15
Sherwood Cl. WA8: Wid 4E 27
Sherwood Cres. WA5: B'wood . . .3C 6
Sherwood Dr. L35: Whis 1B 14
Sherwood Gro. WA6: Hel 2C 60
Shetland Cl. WA2: Fearn 5G 9
WA8: Wid 2E 29
Shevington Cl. WA8: Wid 2E 29
Shevington Wlk. WA8: Wid 2E 29
Shiggins Cl. WA5: Gt San 5H 19
Shillingford Cl. WA4: App 2G 45
Ship St. WA6: Frod 2B 56
Shipton Cl. WA5: W'brk 3F 19
WA8: Wid 2F 27
Shirley Dr. WA4: Grap 3A 34
Shoreham Dr. WA5: Penk 2E 31
Shorewell Cl. WA5: Gt San 4A 18
Short St. WA8: Wid 2A 40
Shorwell Cl. WA5: Gt San 4A 18
Shotwick-Helsby By-Pass
CH2: Elt, Lit Stan, Thor M
. . . . .3A 58
Shrewsbury St. WA4: Warr 2F 33
Shropshire Cl. WA1: W'ston 5E 23
Side Kerfoot St. WA2: Warr 4C 20
Sidings Ct. WA1: Warr 5E 21
Sidmouth Cl. WA5: Penk 1C 30
Silkstone Cres. WA7: Pal F 2H 51
Silverdale Cl. WA6: Frod 4C 56
Silverdale Rd. WA4: Warr 3D 32
Silver La. WA3: Ris 2E 11
(not continuous)
Silver St. WA2: Warr 5D 20
Simkin Av. WA4: Westy 1H 33
SIMM'S CROSS 5B 28
Simonside WA8: Wid 3E 27
Simons La. WA6: Frod 5B 56
Sinclair Av. WA2: Warr 1D 20
WA8: Wid 5H 27
Six Acre Gdns. WA4: Moore 2E 43
Six Acre La. WA4: Moore 2E 43
Sixpenny Wlk. WA1: Warr 5E 21
Skeffington L35: Whis 1A 14
Skiddaw Cl. WA7: Beech 5G 51
Skye Cl. WA8: Wid 2E 29
Slater St. WA4: Warr 1E 33
Slutchers La. WA1: Warr 1C 32
Small Av. WA2: Warr 1E 21
Small Cres. WA2: Warr 1E 21
Smith Ct. WA1: P'ton 4H 21
Smith Cres. WA2: Warr 3F 21
Smith Dr. WA2: Warr 3F 21
Smithills Cl. WA3: Bchwd 4D 10
Smith Rd. WA8: Wid 6H 27
Smith St. WA1: Warr 6D 20
Smithy Brow WA3: Croft 2H 9
Smithy Cl. WA8: Cron 6E 15
Smithy La. WA3: Croft 1A 10
WA6: Hel 6E 55
WA6: K'ley 5G 57
WA8: Cron 5E 15
Smyth Rd. WA8: Wid 3D 28
Snaefell Ri. WA4: App 6E 33
Snowberry Cl. WA8: Wid 1E 29
Snowdon Cl. WA5: Gt San 5C 18
Snowdrop Cl. WA7: Beech 5F 51
Solway Cl. WA2: Fearn 5H 9
Solway Gro. WA7: Beech 4D 50
Somerford Wlk. *WA8: Wid 2E 29*
(off Barneston Rd.)
Somerset Cl. M44: Cad 3H 13
Somerset Way WA1: W'ston 3B 22
Somerville Rd. WA8: Wid 5F 27
Sorbus Cl. CH2: Elt 2G 59
Sorrel Cl. WA2: P'gate 1C 22
Southampton Way
WA7: Murd 3C 52
South Av. WA2: Warr 3D 20
WA4: S Hth 4E 33
Sth. Bank Ter. WA7: Run 4H 39
South Dale WA5: Penk 6D 18
Southdale Rd. WA1: P'ton 4A 22
Southern St. WA4: S Hth 4E 33
Southey Cl. WA8: Wid 5H 27
Southfields Av. WA5: Gt San . . .5D 18
South Front L35: Whis 3A 14
Southlands Av. WA5: Penk 2D 30
Southlands M. WA7: Run 6H 39
South La. WA8: Wid 6E 17
South La. Entry WA8: Wid 1F 29
South Pde. WA7: West P 2F 49
South Rd. WA7: West P 2F 49
South St. WA8: Wid 5B 28
South Vw. Ter. WA5: Cuerd 3G 29
Southway WA7: Pal F 2F 51
(not continuous)
WA8: Wid 5F 27
Southway Av. WA4: App 6F 33
Southwold Cres.
WA5: Gt San 5B 18
Southwood Av. WA7: Wind H . . .5A 42
Southworth Av. WA5: Warr 3B 20
Southworth La. WA2: Win 2F 9
WA3: Croft 2F 9
Sovereign Cl. WA7: Murd 2B 52
Sovereign Ct. WA3: Bchwd 5C 10
Spark Hall Cl. WA4: S'ton 5G 45
Spark La. WA7: Halt 6F 41
Sparrowhawk Cl. WA7: Pal F . . .2G 51
Speakman St. WA7: Run 4H 39
Speedkarting 1B 32
Speke Rd. WA8: Wid 6D 26
Spennymoor Ct. WA7: Pal F 2E 51
Spenser Cl. WA8: Wid 4H 27
Spike Island Vis. Cen. 2A 40
Spinnaker Cl. WA7: Murd 3B 52
Spinners Pl. WA1: Warr 5E 21
Spinney Av. WA8: Wid 4C 26
Spinney Gdns. WA4: App T 3B 46
Spinney Wlk. WA7: Cas 6G 41
Spires Gdns. WA2: Win 2C 8
Springbank Cl. WA7: Run 3B 50
Springbank Gdns.
WA13: Lymm 6F 25
Springbourne WA6: Frod 5D 56
Springburn Gdns.
WA1: W'ston 4F 23
Spring Ct. WA7: Run 5B 40
Springfield Av. WA1: P'gate 3H 21
WA4: Grap 2B 34
WA6: Hel 2D 60
WA13: Lymm 6F 25
Springfield Rd. WA8: Wid 5C 26
Springfields WA6: Hel 2D 60
Springfield St. WA1: Warr 6C 20
Springholm Dr. WA4: App 4F 45
Spring La. WA3: Croft 3B 10
WA13: Lymm 2H 37
Spring St. WA8: Wid 1A 40
Spruce Cl. WA1: W'ston 4E 23
Spurling Rd. WA5: B'wood 3D 6
Square, The WA13: Lymm 2C 36
Squires Av. WA8: Wid 4H 27
Stafford Rd. WA4: Warr 3E 33
Stage La. WA13: Lymm 1F 37
Staines Cl. WA4: App 2G 45
Stainforth Cl. WA3: Cul 3D 4
Stainmore Cl. WA3: Bchwd 3H 11
Stamford Ct. WA13: Lymm 2C 36
Standish Ct. WA8: Wid 5F 27
Stanley Av. WA4: S Hth 3H 33
WA5: Gt San 4B 18
Stanley Cl. WA8: Wid 3C 28
Stanley Pl. WA4: S Hth 3H 33
Stanley St. WA1: Warr 1D 32
WA7: Run 4B 40
Stanley Vs. WA7: Run 6H 39
STANLOW 1A 58
Stanlow & Thornton Station (Rail)
. . . . .1C 58
Stanmore Rd. WA7: Run 5D 40
Stanner Cl. WA5: Call 1H 19
Stansfield Av. WA1: Warr 5H 21
Stansfield Dr. WA4: Grap 6A 34
Stanstead Av. WA5: Penk 2D 30
Stanton Rd. WA4: Thel 2D 34
Stanwood Gdns. L35: Whis 1A 14
Stapleton Av. WA2: Warr 3F 21
Stapleton Ct. WA6: Frod 3C 56
Stapleton Way WA8: Hale B 2D 38
Stapley Cl. WA7: Run 6H 39
Starkey Gro. WA4: Westy 1H 33
Star La. WA13: Lymm 1A 36
Starling Cl. WA7: Murd 2B 52
STATHAM 1B 36
Statham Av. WA2: Warr 1E 21
WA13: Lymm 2A 36
Statham Cl. WA13: Lymm 2B 36
Statham Dr. WA13: Lymm 2B 36
Statham La. WA3: Rix 4G 23
WA13: Lymm 6H 23
Station Av. WA6: Hel 1D 60
Station Rd. CH2: Elt 1F 59
CH2: Ince 1E 59
WA4: Latch 3G 33
WA5: Gt San 6D 18
WA5: Penk 2B 30
WA7: Run 5H 39
WA7: Sut W 5H 51
WA8: Wid 1C 28
Station Rd. Ind. Est.
WA4: Latch 3H 33
Station Rd. Nth. WA2: Fearn . . .1A 22
Station Rd. Sth. WA2: P'gate . . .2A 22
Steel St. WA1: Warr 4F 21
Stenhills Cres. WA7: Run 5C 40
Stephen's Gro. WA6: Hel 3D 60
Stephen St. WA1: Warr 5F 21
Stetchworth Rd. WA4: Walt 4D 32
Steventon WA7: Nort 4B 42
Stewards Av. WA8: Wid 5H 27
Stirling Cl. WA1: W'ston 4E 23
Stirrup Cl. WA2: Fearn 6A 10
Stockdale Dr. WA5: Gt San 3C 18
Stockham Cl. WA7: Halt 1G 51
Stockham La.
WA7: Brook, Halt, Pal F . . .1G 51
(not continuous)
Stockham Lodge Racquet &
Health Club 2H 51
Stockport Rd.
WA4: Grap, Thel 3C 34
Stocks La.
WA5: Gt San, Penk 6B 18
Stockswell Farm Ct.
WA8: Wid 1G 27
Stockswell Rd. WA8: Wid 1B 26
STOCKTON HEATH 4F 33
Stockton La. WA4: Grap 4G 33
Stockton Vw. WA4: Warr 3D 32
Stokes St. WA3: Ris 4E 11
Stoneacre Gdns. WA4: App 3G 45
Stone Barn La. WA7: Pal F 3F 51
Stonechat Cl. WA7: Beech 4F 51
Stonecrop Cl. WA3: Bchwd 5C 10
WA7: Beech 4F 51
Stone Cross Dr. WA8: Wid 6G 15
Stonecross Dr. L35: R'hill 2F 15
Stonehaven Dr. WA2: Fearn 6A 10
Stonehill Cl. WA4: App 3F 45
Stonehills Ct. WA7: Run 5C 40
Stonehills La. WA7: Run 5C 40
Stonelea WA7: Wind H 6H 41
Stoneleigh Ct. WA4: Grap 4D 34
Stoneleigh Gdns. WA4: Grap . . .4D 34
Stone Pit La. WA3: Croft 5A 4
Stoney La. L35: R'hill, Whis 1D 14
Stony Holt WA7: Nort 1A 52
Stonyhurst Cres. WA3: Cul 2D 4
Straight Length WA6: Frod 3F 55
Stratton Cl. WA7: Brook 3H 51
Stratton Pk. WA8: Wid 6H 15
Stratton Rd. WA5: Gt San 6F 19
Strawberry Cl. WA3: Bchwd 5C 10
Stretton Grn. Distribution Pk.
WA4: App T 3D 46
Stretton Rd.
WA4: App T, S'ton 5F 45
Strickland Cl. WA4: Grap 6A 34
Stringer Cres. WA4: Westy 1G 33

A-Z Warrington 77